TO THE POINT
CONFRONTING YOUTH ISSUES

RELIGIONS
Encountering People of Other Faiths

Abingdon Press
Nashville

Table of Contents

Introductions

When Someone Comes to You

Programs

Teaching Articles

Christian Religious Expressions

Other North American Traditions

Easy Reference

A Word from the Editors

The world is no longer (if indeed it ever was) a collection of distinct nations, each with its own particular language, culture, and religion. With the rise of immigration all over the globe, the United States and other nations are facing major changes in language, culture, ethnicity, race, and religion. Teens today live in an environment more multicultural than the world in which their parents and grandparents grew up. *To the Point: Religions* is for Christian youth and adults in the United States. Its purpose is to help them understand their own faith in the context of a multireligious world.

The Shrinking World

The world seems to be shrinking, and it is not only because of the media. Yes, events half a world away blink across our TV screens as they happen. But also our neighborhoods, schools, businesses, and churches have become microcosms of the world. Todays' youth have friends and acquaintances from Japan, Korea, Zimbabwe, Mexico, the Caribbean, India, Iran, Romania. The United States is not a melting pot any longer; it is a nation of nations, as each person expresses the culture, language, and religious beliefs of his or her heritage. At our best, we search for ways to coexist and to cooperate, while retaining the cultural identities that are a cherished part of ourselves and our heritage.

We Are Missionaries

Like Christianity, other religions have a history of missionary endeavors. For centuries, European and then North American Christians have traversed the continents bringing to other people (and sometimes forcing on them) Christian doctrine and beliefs. Why are we surprised to learn that other religious groups have come to the United States as immigrants and missionaries? In North America, there are almost as many Muslims as Presbyterians. Some religious groups, such as the Mormons, have their origins in the United States and have spread out to other parts of the world.

History shows us that a certain amount of fear, as well as intrigue and transformation, are natural responses to exposure to new religions. Even religions that do not seek converts are often viewed with suspicion, simply because they are unknown or different.

Unknown and Different

The United States has laws about the separation of church and state. They guarantee people freedom to worship without the aid or interference of the federal government. Some of us can neatly separate our religious beliefs from our secular lives. For others of us, religious conviction is a part of who we are; our beliefs and actions are intertwined.

When we do not understand what other people believe or how their beliefs influence their actions, we may perceive them as dangerous, mysterious strangers. Teens who are part of religious groups that are indigenous to the United States, such as Jehovah's Witnesses, may be forbidden to participate in the activities of other Christian teens—for example, they may not be able to observe particular religious holidays. On the other hand, they may be active missionaries for their own churches and may seek to persuade other teens to join. Christian groups encourage members to invite others into their religious fellowships as well.

The Challenge

Why are we offering a resource on religions? We have hinted at several reasons. Teens are in a formative time in their lives when they examine, challenge, reexamine, discard, adopt, adapt, and accept many ideas, beliefs, and practices. Religious beliefs are often a prime target for teenagers' evaluation.

Some youth, regardless of the extent or quality of their religious upbringing or their education in the church, may try on different beliefs just to see if they fit. They may see accepting Mom and Dad's Protestant beliefs as one option among many. Youth understand what it means to shop around, and they may choose to shop around for a religion as they would for a product or service.

Other youth may feel threatened by religious proselytizing. They may fear the terrorist actions of extreme religious groups and feel unable to separate what they hear on the news from the beliefs of people they know.

Other youth may choose to drift or to drop out, thinking that religion is irrelevant.

To the Point: Religions Is for You

This resource is designed to help Protestant youth claim Christian faith in the midst of religious diversity. It will help them to appreciate what other people believe and to grapple with ways to respond, from a Christian perspective, to other religions. As our world grows more complex and diverse, youth need and want to know who they are and how they can get along in the world. *To the Point: Religions* will provide some help on the way.

Diana L. Hynson
Anne B. Crumpler

How to Use this Resource

Religious belief is a critical issue for youth today. You may hear about the issue when a teenager says that someone at school is weird because he or she is always talking about God. Or you may know a teen who is open about his or her faith and is criticized, ridiculed, or shunned by other people. Some teens may limit their interaction with other people because of religious restrictions. Others who have been challenged to embrace a new and different set of beliefs may be puzzled about how to respond; other Christian teens may scandalize their parents by looking into non-Christian religions. One basic question is, How can teens understand their own religion and also get along with people from a host of different religious traditions?

The issue is made more complex by the consumer mentality prevalent in the culture of the United States. Youth and adults think it's OK to shop around for a new religion if the old one seems irrelevant or boring.

Teens are ripe for taking on religious challenges. As an adult who works with youth, you will want to help teenagers understand, appreciate, and integrate their Christian beliefs and actions without having to fear, criticize, change, or shun people who believe differently.

To the Point: Religions
Helps You Help Others

Perhaps one of the most poignant and difficult tasks for you, as an adult friend of teens, is helping youth when they are confused, challenged, afraid, or frustrated. The section "When Someone Comes to You" will help you find ways of talking with teens about critical issues. It will provide hints and insights on how to listen effectively and how to be a faithful Christian guide. "When Someone Comes to You" will address theological reflection, discussion skills, and openness to conversation. For example, the section includes information on how to begin and sustain a discussion. It will also explore some of the dynamics of fear that alternative religious viewpoints may elicit in teenagers. "When Someone Comes to You" is the first section; read it before you read the others.

To the Point: Religions
Offers Ready-Made Programs

If you want to offer a program or a series of programs to your youth fellowship group, in a retreat setting, or in a regular class, the "Programs" section is the place to begin. Each program gives you at least forty minutes of discussion, activities, games, and other options for an organized learning experience. The teaching articles can easily be adapted for use with your class.

The writers and editors of *To the Point: Religions* assume and encourage a Christian and Protestant point of view, though they recognize that no one particular set of beliefs is acceptable to all Christians. Both the programs and the teaching articles encourage respect for other religious viewpoints while upholding the Christian faith as normative for people who will use the publication. Our goal is to teach youth and adult workers with youth about a variety of religions, while helping them to claim and maintain their Christian faith.

To the Point: Religions
Seizes Teachable Moments

Not every question about religious viewpoints requires a full-length program. Youth ask casual questions. They may pop in for a visit at your office to ask about something that happened at school. You may receive an anguished call from a parent or guardian about crazy ideas a teen has brought home. How do you respond?

The section "Teaching Articles" provides a wealth of information about different religions, denominations, and belief systems that teens may encounter in their neighborhoods or schools. Each teaching article is presented in a respectful way that attempts to let the religion speak for itself. The articles also include teaching and learning options that will help the student sort out each belief system and often compare it to Protestant Christianity.

As Christians, we do not want to bash other religious systems. We do need to help youth understand, claim, maintain, and integrate their beliefs and actions in a life of Christian discipleship. We can nurture their growth by making other religious systems less mystifying and by providing ways for youth to unpack the Christian faith. Use "Teaching Articles" as a reference for yourself and as a source of study and reflection questions and activities for teens and their parents.

To the Point: Religions
Offers Reference Material

The section "Easy Reference" begins on page 108. The glossary provides ready reference to names, places, figures, scriptures, and terms related to each of the six major religions. If you're interested in facts and figures, there is a statistical chart as well.

What Is Religion?

Religion is a universal human experience. Although not all people participate in an organized religion, every human culture has developed a religion. There are many different religions, but some characteristics are common to them all.

There Is More to Reality than the Physical

In every religion, the spiritual reality is considered to be more real, true, and valuable than the physical world. People refer to the spiritual reality by a variety of names—Supreme Being, Allah, Jehovah—but all agree that the spiritual reality is the foundation, the source, and the essence of the universe and of life itself. Christians call the spiritual reality God.

Life Isn't What It Ought to Be

Religious people claim that the world we live in and human existence are not what they are intended to be. Life in this world is imperfect and needs to be transformed. People speak of the world's imperfection in at least three major ways:

■ *Sin*. The world was created by God, but is presently in a fallen state. Human beings turn away from God, disobey God, violate God's will and law, and seek their own selfish ends. Christians understand sin as the basic human problem.

■ *Ignorance*. Human beings do not know or understand the truth. They do not know the difference between real and unreal, true and false, right and wrong.

■ *Pollution*. Human beings become physically, spiritually, and morally polluted or contaminated by contact with people and things that are impure. They cannot draw near the pure God or Reality; and because of their impurity, they are separated from the good, the true, and the beautiful.

Problems Can Be Overcome

Religious people believe that no matter how great the world's imperfections, they can be overcome; and life can be made better or right, if not perfect. Salvation can be attained.

■ *Sin and Salvation*. God forgives sinners, removes their guilt, and helps them change and turn away from sinning. Because they are weak and evil, people are unable to save themselves. Salvation is the work of a loving and caring God. Christians believe that salvation is effected by the life, death, and resurrection of Jesus Christ.

■ *Ignorance and Knowledge*. Through study and meditation, people can overcome ignorance and gain knowledge, understanding, and wisdom. This solution assumes that if people know what is right, they will be able and willing to do it.

■ *Pollution and Purification*. One can be purified and cleansed by rituals, such as washing the hands and mouth with water or using salt or fire or other purifying agents. The physical rituals are usually also understood as moral or spiritual cleansing. Once purified, people are able to enter holy places and approach the holy god.

Two Basic Ways to Salvation

■ *Faith in and Devotion to a Higher Power or God*. A person must believe in God; have a personal relationship with God through prayers, rituals, and worship; submit to God; obey God; and receive God's freely given blessings. Faith is an attitude of openness and receptivity to God's grace, mercy, and power. Since people are unable to save themselves, they must rely on the grace of God.

■ *Good Works*. People must exert the energy and effort to do good deeds in order to prove themselves worthy of salvation, to gain merit and rewards, or to demonstrate their faith in concrete terms. People do not rely on help from outside themselves, but rather assume responsibility for their own salvation and for the improvement of the world.

There Is a Structure of Mutual Beliefs and Ritual

Religious people develop organizations, institutions, and communities of like-minded people who work together to overcome their problems and find salvation. They develop scriptures, theologies, doctrines, and creeds that explain what their religious experiences mean. They explore the ultimate questions of life: Where did I come from? Why am I here? Who am I? Who is God? Who is my neighbor? What is my destiny? They also use rituals, sacraments, prayers, hymns, meditations, and worship to express their religious experience.

Photo by Jean-Claude LeJeune

When Someone Comes to You

When Someone Comes to You

When a teenager trusts you, he or she will come to you with the hope and expectation that you can deal with specific issues he or she presents. Today's teenagers meet and interact with people from a variety of religious traditions, and they will have concerns and questions about what other people believe. What does that mean for you as an adult friend and worker with youth?

Being a Faithful Guide

Current research tells us that many adults and youth in the church have work to do in order to achieve a well-developed faith. So when a teenager comes to you with a knotty question about his or her faith, what do you do? Actually, you have several choices. You may answer the question. You may refer him or her to the pastor, the resident expert in matters of biblical knowledge and theological application. You may say what you know and try to steer clear of areas that you don't understand. You can answer a question with a question. If you don't know an answer, you might even make up a response that sounds good. What is the most honest and faithful way of taking seriously the concerns of the youth who comes to you and of helping him or her to grow in faith?

■ *The good news is that you do not have to have all the answers.* All of us are at some stage in the faith journey and should respond to teenagers with the best of what we know, acknowledging that there is always more to know. Of course, faith is not a goal, but a way of relating and living. We always have room to grow in our relationship to God. Adults who are in ministry with youth are not answer-givers, but faithful guides on the journey of faith.

■ *It is crucial for adults who work with youth to have specific means of personal and corporate worship, study, reflection, and action.* Biblical knowledge is important, not just in itself, but because the biblical witness leads us toward transformation. To be able to recite John 3:16 is good. To understand, appreciate, and live out a Christian response to the gospel message is to go many steps beyond reading or repeating the content of the Bible. As a faithful guide, you will grow as you lead and encourage others in the faith.

Doing God Talk

People of all religions identify and articulate their beliefs; many religions have sacred writings. But not all religious people engage in theological discourse or express their beliefs easily, because the core of their religion is not in belief but in daily application, in a way of life or behavior. So how do you talk to teens about religion?

■ *The most important way you can help teens deal with their religious questions, challenges, and yearnings is to know what you believe.* You do not have to know all the answers, but you do need to wrestle with the questions. Questions and doubts are a gateway to growth because they remind us that God is revealed in new ways and in new circumstances. As we are transformed by a dynamic faith, we continually become new people in Christ, open to deeper insights of the gospel.

■ *As a faithful guide, you can help teens experience and articulate their own faith.* One way to help teens talk about faith is to tell them your own faith story. Help the youth unpack the meaning of their own religious experiences. If the youth were involved in a worship service or a retreat, ask questions such as these: What did you do in the worship service? How many times did you pray? What kinds of prayers did you say? Did you feel connected with God? How did the music affect you? In what ways were the words of the service important to you? What did they teach you or help you feel about the presence of God in your life? Be prepared to talk to the youth about your own perspective without expecting your experience to be normative.

When presented with challenges to Christian faith or questions about another religious group, help the teens examine their own beliefs and assumptions. Find out what they think and help them sort out myth from reality. If, for example, a teen is attracted by a non-Christian religion, ask: What interests or excites you about it? What do adherents of the religion believe about God? about the Bible? about Jesus? What kind of lifestyle do they lead? How does their lifestyle compare with your understanding of Christian living?

■ *Teenagers need practice in expressing what they believe.* A teenager who has been approached or proselytized by a teen from another religion may be confused and afraid; or he or she may be converted, especially if he or she cannot clearly understand and express the tenets of his or her own faith. Evangelism is a respectable activity for people in many religions; but it may be resisted, resented, and viewed as manipulative by others. You can help teens to clarify what they believe and help them to maintain their faith in the midst of challenges. Your openness to talking about God will make their conversations elsewhere easier.

Expressions of faith are not just verbal, nor are they solely for the purposes of evangelism. A mature faith reaches up to God and out to other people. Teens will look to you, among others, to set an example of faithful living. Indeed, what you do may speak louder than what you profess to believe. Both what you do and what you say are important to your role as a faithful friend and guide for youth.

The Dynamics of Fear

So far, our comments have dealt mainly with the not-so-loaded issues of understanding and talking about faith. Talking about faith takes some courage, and it is incumbent on you to provide youth with a safe arena in which to do so. Still, when teenagers face the prospect of expressing their faith, they may have to deal with a number of fears.

■ *"I'll look stupid."* No one wants to appear foolish or ignorant. The mystique that seems to surround religious intelligence often makes us feel that if we can't get it right, we shouldn't talk about faith at all. The interchange of ideas is one of the ways we learn about and explore what we believe. Don't be afraid to say you don't know the answers, and never put down or allow someone else to put down a teenager because his or her questions seem stupid.

■ *"She's telling me that what I believe is wrong. Is something wrong with what I believe?"* When a teen with an immature faith is confronted by new information or an interpretation that challenges what he or she believes, the resulting confusion can be quite disturbing. To be taught that Adam and Eve are mythical figures rather than real human beings or that the story of Jonah is not a historical report but a wonderful, rich parable may contradict what the teen has learned earlier. Some teenagers may wonder, "If that part of my religion is not true, what else is not true? And how do I know what's true and what isn't?" A teenager may come to question his or her own faith because reincarnation or karma or the eightfold path of enlightenment, though not a part of Christianity, makes a lot of sense. The teen may think, "If these beliefs make so much sense to me, how can my religion say that they are wrong?" If the youth feels that he or she must reorganize or rethink what he or she believes, he or she may also become confused about who he or she is. Rethinking faith may also mean reorganizing or rethinking identity.

■ *"I'm just trying to tell him the truth, and he's attacking my beliefs."* Many religions and denominations are missionary in character. Jehovah's Witnesses, for example, must evangelize or witness door to door as a demonstration of faithfulness. Protestant denominations have different interpretations or understandings of the Bible and biblical authority. (Is the Bible literally true? Is it authoritative for our lives?) Teens who are confronted, rejected, or proselytized because of their beliefs about the Bible may experience feelings of irritation, confusion, and fear. Remember your listening and communication skills and use them (see "Keys to Effective Conversation," page 9.)

■ *"I think this religion is neat. Why are you on my case?"* Teenagers may well be attracted to what seems new and novel in another religion. A United Methodist youth may be attracted to Buddhism and the eightfold path to enlightenment. The major religions all look to an ideal of truth and peace; they all espouse a way of spiritual life. The youth may be content to explore and embrace an exciting new religious life, but he or she may also be afraid to tell friends or family for fear of their reaction and rejection. You may be able to help him or her recognize in his or her own religion what he or she is searching for—for example, he or she may find a way to spiritual truth in The United Methodist understanding of sanctification and Christian perfection.

■ *"I'm afraid of them. If I don't believe what they want me to believe, they'll hurt me."* Teens may hold frightening, mythical ideas about other religions. Interpretations based on the media may skew their understanding of typical adherents of other religions. Do Protestants and Catholics, because of the previous conflicts in Northern Ireland, believe one another to be militant murderers? Because of the violence in the Middle East, do all Jews and Muslims regard one another as terrorists? The gospel says that Jesus is the way; do Christian teens in the United States think that anyone who is not Christian holds an empty faith?

To the Point: Religions will present information on religions, denominations, and faith communities around the world. At the same time, it will help Christian teens to examine and embrace their own religious heritage and beliefs without judging or dismissing other religions. As an adult friend and guide, you can lead youth to understand their own beliefs and to explore other religions in ways that reduce their fears and build their faith.

Keys to Effective Conversation

Leading or guiding others in the faith can take many forms. Leadership implies acting, but an important first step is active listening.

Listening Skills

Teenagers need to be heard, taken seriously, and treated with respect. By charging ahead to give them answers, you may ignore crucial, underlying, unspoken issues. Actively listening to what a teenager says and also to what he or she implies is both a skill to be developed and a gift to be offered.

■ *Active listening seeks to understand the intended meaning of what is said.* Sometimes teenagers say what they mean; sometimes they don't. Listening for meaning requires waiting until the teenager has finished speaking before you respond. Hear everything he or she says; do not let your mind wander or work on a response before he or she is done. When necessary, ask questions for clarification. Be sure to wait for cues from the teenager so that you know when to interject a question. Respond only when you are both satisfied that you understand.

■ *Active listening hears feelings, attitudes, and assumptions.* It is not enough to hear words. Sometimes body language speaks louder than words. For instance, when a teen says that he or she doesn't believe in God, what does he or she do? What feelings does he or she express? Does his or her body language express relief? disappointment? anger? conviction? fear? mischief? Is he or she sitting or standing in a posture that is rigid? relaxed? guarded? What is the expression on his or her face? Are you being challenged? Could the teenager's intent be to test your reaction? Is his or her comment a request for information or an announcement of a decision already made? Considering the teenager's behavior will help you assess what is underneath his or her words. The teen's feelings, attitudes, and assumptions are not the only ones that should be examined. As a faithful adult friend, you will also want to monitor your own feelings, attitudes, and assumptions about what the teenager says and how your conversation takes place. Check up on yourself; watch for ways your reaction either shuts down or encourages further conversation.

■ *Active listening suspends judgment, at least for a while.* Pouncing immediately on a teenager's radical comment (such as a comment about his or her disbelief) can be a death sentence for further communication.

Youth must be able to trust you to hear them out, or they will not discuss issues that are important to them.

Your task will be in deciding what, how, and when to respond. While it is crucial that you know your own convictions, it is equally important to know how and when to let the youth explore their own convictions. They may need to challenge your beliefs in order to sort out their own. Leaping in with easy truth or ready answers may teach content, but suspending judgment and encouraging dialogue will assist a young person in finding his or her own answers.

■ *Active listening requires empathy.* Empathy is the ability to identify with and understand someone else's feelings, circumstances, and motivations. Is the teenager talking to you curious? discouraged from questioning? Is he or she in a family that values challenges and new ideas or one that holds rigidly to a particular set of beliefs? Is he or she emotionally needy so that he or she is apt to latch on to belief systems that feed his or her needs? Is he or she so cynical that no news is Good News? Is he or she self-assured enough to discuss religious beliefs without feeling attacked or foolish?

Revealing and discussing religious beliefs and feelings requires not only interest, but courage. We know that teens yearn for spiritual relationships and that they are curious about nonChristian expressions of faith. It is imperative that caring adults cultivate a secure atmosphere in which teens feel they can express themselves without fear of criticism and without feeling stupid or uncool.

Cultivating Dialogue

The same tools that facilitate active listening cultivate open dialogue. By developing the art of asking questions, you can keep the conversation going. There are four kinds of questions: informational, affective, interpretive, and analytical.

■ *Informational questions ask for content.* What is the name of the founder of Islam? Who were the twelve disciples? What happens at a Bas Mitzvah?

Informational questions are the least intimidating because they ask for the lowest level of personal investment. Questions of content usually have right answers, sometimes several different right answers. When we discuss matters of faith and belief, it is important to know the facts; but the facts are not enough if faith is to be sufficient for life.

■ *Affective questions examine feelings.* How would you feel if Jesus called you to give up everything and to follow him? How do you think Joseph Smith felt when he was persecuted in New York? How did you feel when your comment was criticized by another person in the class?

Answers to affective questions are expressions of feeling and are not right or wrong. We feel what we feel. Because affective questions ask for a personal investment, they may need to be handled carefully. We make commitments to and are transformed by beliefs and practices that touch our hearts as well as our minds.

■ *Interpretive questions draw out implications and relate belief to practice.* What are characteristics of a faithful Hindu? If you took seriously Jesus' mandate to feed the hungry and visit the prisoners, what changes would you make in your life? How do the actions of one religious extremist affect your understanding of other people in his or her religious community?

Questions of interpretation engage our imagination. Part of interpretation may require a knowledge of content, but envisioning possible answers to interpretive questions will help teens relate the beliefs and commitments of their own faith. When they are well-grounded in their own religion, they may expand the limits of their understanding and appreciate new ideas.

■ *Analytical questions examine the relationship between ideas, concepts, practices.* How is the noble eightfold path of Buddhism like Jesus' expectations of his disciples? How is it different? How do Jewish people understand the value of life? How does their understanding compare with that of other religions?

Analysis helps us to look at part of an idea or concept in relationship to the whole and to identify similarities and differences among ideas, practices, and so on. As such, analysis is sometimes impersonal. It is also personal because it allows us to identify myths or fuzzy thinking. A teenager may be enamored of the Hindu idea of reincarnation and also believe in the Resurrection.

How can you, as a faithful guide, help him or her to see whether his or her beliefs hang together?

■ *The ways we ask questions and phrase our remarks can avoid conversational pitfalls.* Saying yes or no or asking questions that require yes or no answers (for example, Do Christians believe that Jesus is the Son of God?) leads quickly to a conversational dead end. Likewise, questions and comments that imply bias, suggest particular answers, or appear judgmental will end a conversation. Some questions ask for no response and may well embarrass or anger the youth: You don't really believe that, do you? You don't really believe that ridiculous notion, do you? Biased questions (for example, Don't you think that the Bible is the literal and infallible word of God?) tend to limit the imagination and the conversation. Removing bias (How do you understand and interpret God's word in the Bible?) opens up the conversation to new possibilities. Neutral comments, such as, "Say more about that," draw out the teenager and allow him or her the freedom to answer in his or her own way.

Younger youth are just beginning to think abstractly. In conversation, you may want to offer suggestions or choices that limit their answers but also offer a frame of reference that will help them see the range of possible answers. You might ask questions such as these: If Jesus asked you to you leave your family to follow him, would you feel scared? angry? excited? confused? lonesome? irritated? privileged? Or you might say, Jews and Muslims regard Jesus as a wise, human prophet; and Christians believe he is God in the flesh. What do you think? Why?

We all know that some youth will say or do things just to see how you respond. Whether and how you react will help determine the course of the conversation. Always remember that even when a teenager is testing or teasing you, he or she may be more fragile that you think. Questions or comments, especially about something as intimate as his or her faith, should be answered with care. However, an appropriate sense of humor will enhance your relationships with youth and will keep you from taking yourself too seriously.

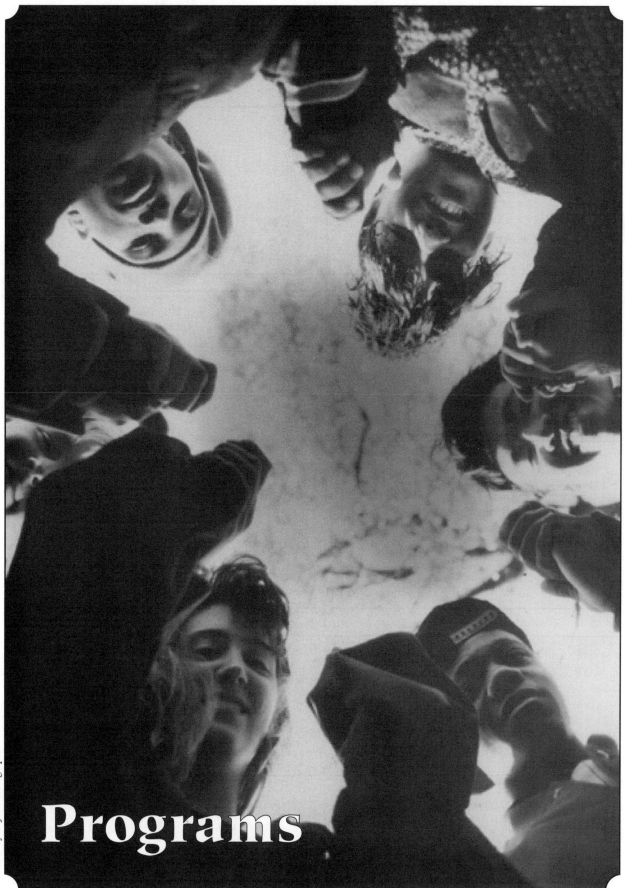

Photo by Skjold Photographs

Programs

Standing on Solid Ground

PURPOSE: To assist youth in identifying and sustaining what they believe, even when they don't agree with other people or when others don't agree with them.

Preparation

➤ Have available Bibles; commentaries on Genesis, Luke, John, and Acts; hymnals; paper and pencils; large sheets of paper and felt-tip markers; old magazines; scissors; and glue.

➤ Obtain a copy of *Childrens Letters to God: The New Collection*, by Stuart Hample and Eric Marshall (Workman Publishing, 1991). Select letters to use in the activity, "Dear God . . ."

Who Am I?

➤ Say to the group: "Most of us take a lifetime to find out who we are and what we believe. This lesson is about how to find out and how to stand up for what we believe."

➤ Ask the youth to read aloud The Apostles' Creed. Explain that The Apostles' Creed is one way the church has expressed its faith through the centuries.

➤ Sometimes a story captures what we believe better than a sermon or lecture. Assign one of the following passages to each person or small discussion group. Distribute commentaries so that group members can find out more about the passages.

Luke 12:4-12 (value and responsibilities of disciples)
Luke 12:13-21 (priorities)
Luke 11:37-54 (hypocritical leaders)
Genesis 11:1-9 (confusion of speech)
Acts 2:1-21 (understanding of language)
John 3:1-21 (salvation of humankind)

➤ Ask the following questions about each reading:

What does the story say about the characters in the story?

What does it say about the person who believes?

Why, do you think, was the story included in a sacred writing?

Which story best describes you? Why? Which story best describes your approach to faith? Why?

I Think I Believe

➤ Invite the group to write a creed, or statement of belief. Members of the group should consider these questions:

Do you believe in God?

What do you believe about God?

What does God do for people?

Who is Jesus? What is Jesus' role in our faith?

Do you believe in salvation?

How does God save people?

Who is the Holy Spirit? What is the role of the Holy Spirit in our faith?

How do you experience God in your life?

I Don't Know What to Ask

➤ Ask *younger youth* to read **Genesis 32:22-32** and to look it up in a commentary. Encourage the group to include information from the commentary in their discussion of these questions:

Jacob was wrestling with God; what did he want from God?

Why was a name so important? How would knowing the name have been a blessing to Jacob?

Did Jacob get what he wanted?

➤ Ask *older youth* to read **John 20:24-29**, to research it in the commentary, and then to discuss the following questions:

Why didn't Thomas believe that Jesus had been raised?

What did Thomas want from Jesus? Did he get it?

Was it OK with Jesus for Thomas to have doubts?

What was it about Jesus that Thomas had a hard time believing? How was Thomas's picture of Jesus different from Jesus' picture of himself?

Dear God . . .

➤ Bring together the older and younger youth. Read aloud the letters you have selected from *Children's Letters to God: The New Collection.*

➤ Ask the youth to imagine that they are God and to answer the children's questions. Write the group's answers on a chalkboard or on large sheets of paper. Some of their responses will probably be silly; others will be serious. Invite the youth to discuss the picture of God that emerges from their answers.

➤ Then ask the group members to list questions they would ask God if they were offered an opportunity to do so.

How Do I Get Some Answers?

➤ Invite the teens to make a list of at least fifteen church people that they can ask religious questions. Then tell them to elect one of the fifteen to each of the following categories:

■ most likely to give them deep and thoughtful answers
■ most likely to ask them why they're asking
■ most likely to give them a hug with the answer
■ most likely to tell a story with the answer
■ most likely to ask them to explain to the whole class
■ most likely to show them how to look it up themselves

Helpful Hints for Study and Reflection

■ Read a Bible that has notes, cross-references to other passages, a concordance, maps, and other study aids.

■ Read a commentary after you read and reflect on the Scripture. Some commentaries are highly technical, but many are written for interested laypeople. Ask your pastor, look in the church or local library, or check with your denomination's bookstore for help finding a good commentary.

■ Use Bible dictionaries, maps, and concordances.

■ Ask yourself questions about the context of the passage. What are the main events? Who is involved? What are the secondary events? Who is not included? What are possible consequences? What actually happened? Who was affected and how? How does the Scripture apply to my life?

■ Read the other articles in this book, especially the ones on Christianity and on expressions of the Christian faith. (See the table of contents.)

What if I Can't Believe What Somebody I Love Believes?

➤ Invite the youth to discuss "Ryan's Story" (on page 14) or one or more of the following scenarios:

■ Your parents are evangelical, born-again Christians who believe that people must believe in Christ to be saved. Your boyfriend or girlfriend is a Buddhist, and you are attracted to his or her religion. You are thinking of becoming a Buddhist. What will you tell your parents? How will they react? Explain your answers.

■ Your pastor preaches about accepting things, like homosexuality, that you think are wrong. Your congregation recently voted to openly accept and welcome gays. You love your church, but you feel torn. What will you do? Is it OK to shop around for a new church because you disagree with something your church has done? Explain your answers.

■ Your friend in school is a member of a Christian denomination that believes that only baptism in the denomination will save a person from going to hell. How does his or her belief change your friendship? Do you want to join his or her church so that you can be saved? How will you and your friend resolve the problem? Explain your answers.

■ You have a friend who wears a turban all the time. He is from India and a Sikh. He never cuts his hair. Several of your friends and even your brothers and sisters make fun of him and call him names. You wonder why he can't cut his hair and live like a normal American. Why is the turban such a big deal? How will you deal with the fact that he embarrasses you? Explain your answers.

For more information see
"Four Stairways to Heaven" on pages 20-23.

Ryan's Story

Ryan was an average American 15-year-old. He went to a public school, which he hated because the people were weird and the teachers were mean old fogies. Ryan was taking driver's education this year. He couldn't wait until he could drive.

Janie was also an average American 15-year-old. She went to the same school Ryan attended, and she also hated it. However, Janie's reasons for hating school were different from Ryan's. Janie was a Pentecostal. She was not allowed to cut her hair; she wore it long, pulled back with a tie, or in a bun on top of her head. She had to wear dresses that came below her knees. Her faith taught her that it was a sin for a woman to dress like a man, so she couldn't wear jeans. And appearing sexy was the worst kind of sin: a violation of her duty to God.

Ryan made fun of Janie. He sat behind her in geometry and pulled her hair, kicked her chair, and pinched her whenever he got the chance. When she protested, Ryan would laugh and say, "Janie, lighten up. Doesn't your Bible say, 'Be fruitful and multiply'? I'd like to multiply with you, babe." When Janie told a teacher, she shrugged and said, "Boys will be boys." And the school administration had bigger problems to worry about. After Janie complained, Ryan's taunts and harassment would only get worse.

Ryan was also a Christian. He attended the United Methodist church down the road from Janie's Pentecostal church. That's how he knew what the Bible said about being fruitful. Unfortunately, he forgot to read the part about loving neighbors.

Janie's family eventually had her moved to another class, away from Ryan. The harassment eased. Still whenever Ryan saw Janie in the hall, he would get his friends to make fun of her and he would grab at her as she went by.

➤ Invite the class to discuss these questions about the story:

Was Ryan wrong? Why? Why not?

Was Ryan wrong because he sexually harassed Janie or because he made fun of her religion? Is one more wrong than the other? Why?

Should Janie have dressed differently in order to avoid harassment? Why? Why not? Why do some religious groups have restrictions or requirements about the way their members dress or wear their hair?

If you were Janie, how would you feel about your religion? What would you think and how would you feel about Ryan's religion?

What do Ryan's actions say about his system of beliefs? Would Ryan's religious beliefs allow him to mistreat Janie? Why? Why not?

Is it more important to fit in or to be faithful? Is it ever OK to make fun of somebody's religion?

Standing Up for My Faith

➤ Choose four youth to play the following roles:

■ MELISSA: an Anglo-American fourteen-year-old, who is Roman Catholic;

■ RAUL: an Hispanic-American sixteen-year-old, who is an evangelical Christian;

■ SOON-HEE: a fifteen-year-old citizen of Korea, living in America during high school. She is a Buddhist;

■ PHILLIPE: a fourteen-year-old French immigrant whose family is applying for American citizenship. He is a convert to Islam.

➤ Ask the four youth to act out the following dialogue and to roleplay an ending to the story:

MELISSA: I hate history class. Whoever wrote the book seems to think that Europeans are the creators of civilization and the saviors of the world. Some explorer sails to a new place, decides the native people are savages, and converts them to Christ—or kills them. And the church supports him!

RAUL: What about Christopher Columbus? He introduced the Americas to Europe. That's got to count for something. It wasn't his fault that he brought all those diseases with him and wiped out half the Indian population. How could he know?

SOON-HEE: I suppose you think that's OK because the conquerors were Christian or because it happened so long ago. Not too long ago, the Communist Party tried to eliminate my religion in Korea. When you're on the receiving end, things look a lot different.

PHILLIPE: Christians wanted to take over the Muslim world centuries ago, even though we were a more sophisticated and cultured people. We held them off for about four hundred years and went out fighting. If the Indians didn't like what was happening to them, they should have done something to stop it. Muslims want peace, but if anyone threatens us or the true religion, we know Allah will help us fight back.

RAUL: From what I've seen on the news, all you Muslims think about is killing your enemies. Jesus Christ is the Prince of Peace. Columbus might have thought the Indians were savages, but I can think of a better example.

SOON-HEE: What do you know about peace and harmony? You Christians have a bloody history. And what about the televangelists who scream for money and hop from one scandal to the next?

MELISSA: Christians commit sins like everyone else, but we can rely on God. Looking inside for enlightenment might be the latest in pop psychology, but only God can save us.

PHILLIPE: Some Muslims are extremists; and only the extremists make the news. The rest of us follow Allah peacefully. You don't have to like us. We do what we do, and we know that our devotion to Allah is all we need.

➤ Invite the group to discuss these questions:

With which of the teenagers' beliefs and attitudes do you agree? disagree?

Which teens have a positive view of their own religion? of another religion?

Is it possible to be a Christian and let other people believe what they will? Why? Why not?

Is putting down another person's beliefs an appropriate way to express your own faith? Why? Why not?

Melissa and Raul are both Christians. Do they agree with each other? In order to be considered faithful, should all Christians agree? Why? Why not?

Read **John 3:16-18.** Do people have to believe in Jesus in order to be saved? Why? Why not?

How can you stand up for what you believe without condemning another person's religion?

Facing Helps and Hurts

➤ Ask the youth to reflect on these questions:

What keeps you from standing up for what you believe?

What tempts you to wimp out when you are confronted about your faith?

➤ Ask the participants to name three obstacles to standing up for what they believe.

➤ Then ask them to make a list of things they can do to help themselves stand up for what they believe.

➤ Draw a line down the center of a long sheet of paper. Write on one side "Helpers" and on the other side "Hurters." Distribute magazines. Ask the youth to cut out pictures of things that help or hurt their faith and to tape or glue the pictures to the paper. They may choose to complete the collage by drawing or writing about things that help or hurt their faith.

If You Have More Time

➤ Invite the group to practice ways of responding to the teenagers in the roleplay (Melissa, Raul, Phillipe, Soon-Hee). Ask the participants to consider these questions:

What would you say about your faith and beliefs?

How would you respond to each of the people in the roleplay? What would you say about his or her beliefs?

What does your religion ask of you when you encounter people whose beliefs are different from your own?

Worship

➤ Invite the participants to read aloud their creed.

➤ Ask the group to sing "Stand Up for Jesus" or another hymn about having the courage to follow Jesus Christ.

➤ Pray:

With our hearts and hands and voices, we sing your praises, God of love and life. Teach us to love you as we love each other. Strengthen our faith to withstand the mightiest storm. Even as we are tossed by strong winds, we will call on your name. And at last we will come home to you. Amen.

Religion? Who Cares?

PURPOSE: To examine religious faith that exists in the face of cultural opposition and to support youth who must cope with the culture of disbelief.

Preparation

➤ Gather art supplies for "Who Can Reach Me?" You will need a chalkboard and chalk or large sheets of paper and felt-tip markers.

➤ Have available Bibles, at least one topical concordance, and hymnals for worship.

➤ Read "Interesting Stuff About the Thirteenth Generation." Copy the list and cut apart the statements. Tape or glue each statement to a separate index card.

Who Can Believe All that Stuff?

➤ Ask the participants to form age-level groups.

➤ For *older youth*, describe the culture of disbelief. (See the box on page 17; look also at "Interesting Stuff About the Thirteen Generation" on page 19). Start a discussion using some or all of the following:

■ In the late 1800's, Charles Darwin's theory of evolution rocked the religious community by apparently contradicting the belief that God created the world and everything in it in six days. Do you agree with Darwin? the Bible? Could both be right? Why? Why not? Why is the question of evolution and creation still a hot topic in some religious circles?

■ Many people in both the religious and secular communities thought that the Vietnam conflict was immoral. It lasted eleven years, from 1964 to 1975, and polarized our nation. As a student, President Clinton, a faithful Baptist, protested the war. What have you heard about the opinions of individuals and churches during the Vietnam war? What do you think?

■ The Gulf War lasted less than two months; its style has been described as "get in, get it done, get out." In what ways did the style of the war reflect the values of your faith? of your generation?

■ Prominent slogans such as *Why ask why?* and *Just do it!* reflect the values of the Thirteenth Generation. Christianity teaches that we should rely on God, rather than on ourselves, and that we should seek answers in prayer. In what ways do your values clash with traditional religion? How do you understand the contradictions between traditional religion and the beliefs and values of the Thirteenth Generation?

■ American culture tends to portray religious people as out of touch. What does your pastor say and do to help you find your way in the world? Do you think he or she is out of touch with your culture? Why? Why not?

■ The Constitution of the United States provides for the separation of church and state. We are free to believe (or not) as we choose, and we are not free to impose our faith on others. How does freedom of religion affect you? For example, how do you feel about the campaign to reinstate school prayer?

■ Are some of your friends nonbelievers? Why do they refuse to accept religious beliefs?

■ Teenagers say that religion has less influence on their lives than do friends, home, school, music, and TV. At the same time, forty-two percent of all teenagers say that they frequently pray alone. Are we living in a culture of disbelief? Are you?

➤ For *younger youth*, introduce information about the culture of disbelief (see the box on page 17). Then use the following questions as discussion starters:

Is Bart Simpson a Christian? Does he act like a Christian? Does he express your feelings? Why? Why not?

Do most adults like the Simpsons or dislike them? Why do they like them? dislike them? Why do so many children and teens like the show?

What do adults say or do that shows they understand teenagers? What demonstrates their lack of understanding? Are adults who go to church different from adults who don't go to church? What has been your experience with older Christians?

Why are there differences between teenagers' feelings and adults' feelings? What are the differences?

My Way

➤ Ask the participants to say lines from songs that express their feelings. Then ask the group to read the words of "The Old Rugged Cross" or a similar hymn. Ask these questions:

Which songs best describe your feelings? Which ones are especially meaningful to you? Why?

Which songs dismiss or insult Christianity? Which say that religion is not important?

What attitudes or feelings expressed in the lyrics or music contradict your religious beliefs? In what other ways does the culture contradict religious beliefs?

Is Christian rock an appropriate way of reaching youth with the Christian message? Why? Why not?

➤ Invite participants to write a hymn that reflects Christian beliefs and the teens' values and that uses the tune of "Amazing Grace."

Culture of Disbelief

We live in an age when religion has come under fire. In American culture, religious people are viewed as naive, uninformed, fanatic, or worse. Some people think that faith is not important enough to talk about. How did disbelief and distaste for religion come to be? How will youth survive in a culture of disbelief? How will they learn and grow in faith when so many people don't care?

One challenge to organized religion has come from modern science. During the Enlightenment, over a hundred years ago, science began to explain the universe and people began to question accepted beliefs and religious traditions. They moved from asking how and what to believe to wondering whether and why they should believe at all. If medical technology can keep a person alive, why bother to pray? What does the possibility of growing babies in test tubes say about the role of God in creation? Sophisticated weapons can destroy the world many times over; what's the point in talking about a Prince of Peace? With so much evil in the world, can we even consider the existence of God?

The culture of disbelief insists that questions based on religious belief are the wrong questions. After all God—if there is a God—is either unable or unwilling to take care of the world God created. God doesn't matter; personal power and self-sufficiency are the answers the world is looking for.

Recently, religion—or spirituality—seems to be making a comeback. But what kind of comeback?

No matter what history has served up, people have always yearned for spirituality. People ask basic questions: Why am I? What is the meaning of life? of my life? Who is in charge of the world? And people still want God to be at the center of their lives, even if God is talked about or experienced in ways that are new to religious tradition. What role will religion play in the twenty-first century? What part will religion play in the lives of youth as they come of age?

If you would like to dig deeper into the topic of the culture of disbelief, see *The Culture of Disbelief: How American Law and Politics Trivialize Religious Devotion,* by Stephen L. Carter; BasicBooks, 1993.

Voices

➤ Invite the participants to consider the quotations in "Voices" (see the box on this page). Discuss the following questions:

Which of the quotations reflect your values as a Christian youth? Why?

Which quotations reflect a culture of disbelief or a belief different from your own? Why?

Voices

■ "If they can't say it in a hour, they ought to put it on a tape." (13-year-old Rashad Mobley, on going to church, page 30)

■ "We're a secret generation. Nobody knows what we think." (Bethany Ericson, 22, Brighton, MA, page 11)

■ "I feel stupid and contagious." (song by Nirvana, "Smells Like Teen Spirit," page 16)

■ "The good thing about our generation is you can be gay or straight, with someone your own color or not. Whatever you want." (Brian Rich, 23, San Francisco, page 158)

■ "Don't ask me why I play this music
It's my culture, so naturally I use it"
(song by Living Colour, "Pride," page 183)

■ "It's not the baby boom that's going to fight the next war. It's more likely that the baby boom will start it." (Julie Phillips, "Boomed Out," in *Seattle Weekly*, page 223)

From THE 13TH GENERATION, by Neil Howe and Bill Strauss. Copyright 1993 by Neil Howe and Bill Strauss. Reprinted by permission of Vintage Books, a Division of Random House, Inc.

What Have You Done for Me Lately?

➤ Invite the participants to read and discuss the story "What Have You Done for Me Lately?" (see the box on this page). Use these questions to sustain the conversation:

Is the story realistic? Why? Why not? Is it realistic in a culture that says religion is unimportant?

Do you know anybody whose life is like Kim's? Did he or she have the support of a religious community? If so, what difference did it make?

Are drugs and sex adequate ways of coping with feelings of despair? Do you understand why Kim was tempted?

Would Kim and her family fit in at your church? Why? Why not?

What do religion and Christian faith have to say to Kim?

What good news does Kim's family need to hear from the church? What would help Kim hear the message of hope or faith?

What Have You Done for Me Lately?

Kim was sick of her life. She lived in low-income government housing, her mother was an alcoholic, and she had never met her father. She and her mother and her two younger brothers lived with her grandmother, who worked in a factory twelve hours a day for minimum wage. Kim, though only fourteen, was expected to bring home a paycheck; she delivered papers.

Kim's brother Michael was eleven and in a gang. Though his grandmother didn't know and his mother didn't care if she did know, Michael carried a knife to school every day and sometimes stashed a gun in his backpack. Kim's youngest brother, Nicholas, had a hyperactive disorder that made him run around all the time and do poorly in school.

Because Kim's grandmother was working, the family did not qualify for government assistance. Nicholas' medical condition had been diagnosed by the school, but the family couldn't afford to have it treated.

Kimberly wanted to stop her world and get off for a while.

Kim's family tried to go to church, but the people there did not seem to understand how painful life was for them. The church people arrived in nice cars and wore pretty dresses and suits. The pastor preached about sins that only money could buy—greed, pride, laziness—sins that Kim and her family couldn't even

---

think about. Kim lived in poverty and under constant stress; the church did not touch her life.

As each day brought more despair, Kim lost hope. She was falling into a pit, and nobody could reach out to catch her. By the time Kim turned fifteen, she was hooked on crack cocaine, she was pregnant, and she had lost her job. All she wanted from crack was a chance to forget her life for awhile, and all she wanted from sex was love. She didn't get a moment of peace, and she didn't get love. All she got was more despair.

Why Should I Believe?
Surviving the Culture of Disbelief

➤ Invite the members of the group to name the problems religions ought to address and the questions religious people ought to be able to answer. Write the problems and the questions on a chalkboard or a large sheet of paper.

➤ Provide Bibles and a topical concordance.

➤ Ask the participants to read the scenarios below and on page 19 and to answer these questions:

Does religious faith have anything to do with the issues described in the scenarios? Why? Why not?

In what ways could your faith help the people involved?

How would the situations change if the people involved believed that the Holy Spirit would guide and comfort them?

If their only response to religious belief was, "Who cares?" what would be the consequences of the situations?

As a result of talking about the scenarios, how would you change the list of questions and problems that religious groups should address?

SCENARIOS

■ Mark is flunking out of school because he is angry at his father for putting pressure on him to become a big-time lawyer.

■ Elizabeth keeps getting in fights at school. A group of girls calls her a fat slob because she is a few pounds overweight. Eating helps her cope with hurt feelings, so she continues to gain.

■ Tara is bored to tears with church. Her parents force her to go to worship every Sunday morning and to youth group every Sunday night, but church is a big yawn. It means nothing to her.

■ Rosalina is in love with Josef. They're good friends, and they seem just right for each other. The problem is that Rosalina is Hispanic and Catholic and Josef is Jewish. Both families want the romance stopped.

■ Erin has an eating disorder, though you would never know it. She stuffs herself at meals and then throws up. Stuffing herself with food fills up the empty hole she feels inside, and throwing up keeps her from gaining weight. She thinks it is the perfect solution.

■ Megan is beginning to wonder if she might be a lesbian. She is not attracted to boys in any way. But she has eyes and ears, and she knows how people feel about homosexuality. Every day Megan grows more depressed.

Who Can Reach Me?
Overcoming the Culture of Disbelief

➤ Write on index cards the statements from "Interesting Stuff About the Thirteenth Generation." Distribute the cards so that each person has one. Or divide the class into small groups and give each group a card.

➤ Ask each person or small group to respond to these questions:

Does the statement on your index card describe you? your values? your situation?

What does the church have to say to people described by the statement? What do they need to hear from a pastor or the members of a church?

What are people described by the statement hearing in response to what their lives are like? What's missing? What do they need to hear?

How can people described by the statement ask for what they want or need? Whom can they ask?

Worship

➤ Read aloud **Acts 3:1-10**.

➤ Invite the participants to pray a bidding prayer. The leader will start the prayer and then invite volunteers to say short prayers. After each of the participant's prayers, the leader will say, "Lord in your mercy"; and the group will respond, "Hear our prayer." For example:

Leader: We pray for our country.
Group: (*Individuals will say short prayers for the country.*)
Leader: Lord in your mercy,
Group: Hear our prayer.

➤ Invite the class to sing "Open My Eyes."

Interesting Stuff
About the Thirteenth Generation

■ The Thirteenth Generation includes youth and young adults born between 1961 and 1981.

■ Just over ten percent of all college students take religion courses. Religion ranks ahead of philosophy and below English literature.

■ Sixth to twelfth graders who go to church are half as likely to engage in at-risk behavior—smoking, drugs, premarital sex—as teens who do not attend.

■ Today's teens are like the Lost Generation, born between 1883 and 1900. They are adventurous, mischievous, hard, materialistic, neglected by their parents, labeled with a bad reputation for crime and violence. The Lost Generation despised the generation one step ahead of them, and fiercely protected the one that followed.

■ Because they feel neglected and scorned by their elders, survival is the most important value for today's teenagers.

■ Religion is important for today's youth, but only if it makes sense to them, if it is practical, and if they can see its results.

■ The suicide rate for teens is higher than it has ever been in American history.

■ Most teenagers regard Baby Boomers as self-righteous moralist hypocrites who have sold out.

■ Teenagers today live less by values than by slogans: *Life is short—play hard. Why ask why? Just do it. Just say no.*

■ Several names have been coined for this generation: Baby Busters, Lost Generation, Nowhere Generation, Generation X, and the Bottom Line Generation.

■ In a 1989 Gallup Poll, people ages 18-29 ranked the following values in order of their importance: having an exciting and stimulating life (63%), working for the betterment of society (58%), following a strict moral code (53%), and having a nice home and car (44%).

■ The Thirteenth Generation is religious, but they have sharp noses for hypocrisy. Religion should be simple and free of self-righteous platitudes.

■ Teenagers today watch movies and listen to music from any generation. They can quote lines from movies six decades old.

■ The Thirteenth Generation values trash disposal. They scorn people who don't clean up their own messes because they feel they are stuck with cleaning up the messes left by previous generations. And they still catch the blame for all the problems of the world.

Four Stairways to Heaven

PURPOSE: To examine four approaches to faith that occur in most denominations and in many religions: evangelicalism, liberalism, fundamentalism, and pentecostalism.

Preparation

➤ Distribute paper and pencils. Have available a cardboard box big enough to put over a person's head.

➤ Make a chart. Number from 1 to 5 down the left side of a sheet of paper. Make four columns. Label the columns "Evangelical," "Liberal," "Fundamental," and "Pentecostal." Photocopy the chart so that everyone will have a copy.

➤ Have available Bibles and commentaries for the activity "Rubber Hits the Road."

➤ If the group is not part of a pentecostal church, arrange for them to visit a church service in which the spiritual gifts are practiced.

Four Stairways

This activity looks at four ways of understanding and living faith.

Evangelicals: Just a Closer Walk

➤ Read or summarize the following information about evangelicals:

The Evangelical Movement emerged from the religious awakenings of the 1700s. Although it had its origin in European Protestantism, it grew primarily in America. In the second half of the nineteenth century, industry hit the big time and the American way of life changed forever. Many evangelicals believed that only the second coming of Christ would cure the world's woes. They also believed that Christians were called to personal holiness and a moral life. To be an evangelical is to be a gospel-believer. Evangelicals believe strongly in the authority of the Bible. They believe a person must be born again, that he or she must have a personal conversion experience in Jesus Christ. After a person is born again, he or she will live a moral life marked by personal devotion and a zeal for winning souls for Christ.

TYPES AND GRIPES

➤ Identify the following comments as stereotypes and complaints about evangelicals:

- They are intolerant and bigoted.
- They don't want Christians to think.
- They are racist, sexist, and escapist.
- They invade and disrupt cultures in the name of Christian mission.

ARE YOU AN EVANGELICAL?

➤ Give each person a four-column chart and a pencil. Ask the youth to respond to the following statements by writing "true" or "false" in the column labeled "Evangelical":

1. I believe a Christian must be born again. (2)
2. I believe in a personal walk with Christ. (1)
3. I believe that Christ is the only savior, and that all people must be brought to believe in him. (5)
4. I believe that every word of the Bible is absolutely true. (4)
5. I believe a Christian should live a moral life, and should refrain from premarital sex, smoking, drinking, and other illicit behavior. (3)

➤ The number at the end of each statement indicates the number of points the youth will receive if they think the statement is true. Read all the point values and ask the youth to tally up their points.

Liberals: I'm OK; You're OK

➤ Read or summarize the following information about liberals:

The liberal movement started with the dawn of the Enlightenment and the Industrial Revolution. As science began to claim truth about the world, liberals attempted to change religion so that it would be more in line with scientific truth. Liberals began to question the literal truth of doctrines such as Creation and the virgin birth. They understood that the Bible was a book written before people knew the teachings of science and that the Bible must be interpreted in light of the contemporary world. They did not mean that the Bible should be discarded, but that the variations in ancient and modern culture, history, and scholarship must be taken into account when interpreting Scripture.

The Social Gospel movement emerged as a result of liberalism. A moral Christian is more than a good person; he or she is called to change the sins of the world: racism, sexism, classism, injustice. Tolerance is a source of pride for liberals. They believe in Jesus Christ as the essential model for life, but they also recognize that God may be revealed in other religious expressions and experiences.

TYPES AND GRIPES

➤ Identify the following comments as stereotypes and complaints about liberals:

- They have slipped away from true belief.
- They don't believe in the Bible.
- For them, anything goes; any belief is acceptable.
- Tolerance is another word for lukewarm faith.
- For them, faith is an intellectual exercise.

ARE YOU A LIBERAL?

➤ Ask the youth to respond to the following statements by writing "true" or "false" in the column labeled "Liberal"; then invite them to tally up their points:

1. I believe that faith ought to conform to our scientific and technological world. (3)
2. I believe the Bible must be interpreted; there is more to the Scripture than what appears at face value. (4)
3. I believe that other religions may be true too. (5)
4. I believe that Christians in today's world must think as much as they feel. (1)
5. I believe that certain doctrines and stories such as the virgin birth, Creation, Jonah and the great fish, may illuminate faith, even if they aren't literally true. (2)

Fundamentalists: "Now You've Gone Too Far!"

➤ Read or summarize the following information about fundamentalists:

Fundamentalism emerged from the evangelical movement as a way of refuting liberal or modernist views in religion and faith. Liberals were making dangerous moves toward tolerating what many fundamentalists believed was intolerable. For many fundamentalists, the chief Christian duty is to combat liberal theology and certain secular trends; others hold more moderate opinions. Fundamentalists believe that the return of Christ is just around the corner and that we must be prepared at a moment's notice. They believe that the Bible is literally true and that its prophecies refer to today's world. Winning souls for Christ and church growth are primary concerns for fundamentalists, as they are for evangelicals.

Fundamentalists got their name from a set of booklets called *The Fundamentals: A Testimony to Truth*, published between 1910 and 1915, which outlined the five fundamentals of Christian faith:

- The Bible is the inspired Word of God and is without error of any kind;
- Jesus Christ was God in human flesh;
- Jesus was born of a virgin and lived a sinless life;
- Jesus was the sacrifice substituted for sinful men and women, and his death and resurrection atoned for the sins of all humanity;
- Jesus was physically resurrected and will come again in physical form.

The main difference between fundamentalists and evangelicals is that most fundamentalists are more aggressive in their fight against liberals' influence in faith and politics. Many fundamentalists draw sharp lines between themselves, liberals, and evangelicals who don't believe in their methods. Billy Graham formally separated himself from the fundamentalists after he was called a traitor because he accepted the cooperation of prominent liberal church leaders.

Since the early 1920s, when the fundamentalist movement grew and began to experience internal conflict, the label, fundamentalism, has caused division. Some early evangelicals who reacted to modernist or liberal theology and social policy also reacted to intellectualism. They attacked both the beliefs of liberals and the arenas in which they were discussed: seminaries and universities. Not all fundamentalists are anti-intellectuals or afraid of discussion or debate, but all hold fast to the fundamentals of the faith.

TYPES AND GRIPES

➤ Identify the following comments as stereotypes and complaints about fundamentalists:

- They believe they are right and everybody else is going to hell.
- They believe in a white-male-supremacist version of Christianity.
- They fear and reject people who are known homosexuals.
- They believe any woman who gets an abortion is condemned.
- They want women to stay barefoot and pregnant.

➤ Read each fundamental (The Bible is the inspired Word of God and is without error of any kind, Jesus Christ was God in human flesh, and so on). After each, ask the youth to raise their hands if they believe the statement to be true. Then say to the group: "If you believe the fundamentals, are you a fundamentalist? Not quite. Fundamentalists have changed over the years and have become more involved in fighting the liberal political agenda."

➤ Ask the youth to respond to the following statements by writing "true" or "false" in the column labeled "Fundamental"; then invite them to tally up their points:

1. I believe in all five fundamentals of the Christian faith. (1)
2. I believe the liberal movement must be combatted at every turn. (4)
3. I believe that every word of the Bible is true. (5)
4. I believe that the religious right is just and good in its fight against the liberal agenda. (2)
5. I believe that women should not be ordained as pastors. (3)

Pentecostals: Kissed by the Spirit

➤ Read or summarize the following information about pentecostals:

The Pentecostal Movement began as a holiness movement in the late nineteenth century. Pentecostalism is fairly new and exists in most cultures in the world, except for those dominated by Islam. Pentecostals believe in practicing the spiritual gifts of speaking in tongues; faith healing; casting out demons; and performing miracles, signs, and wonders. The most important part of being a pentecostal is being baptized in the Spirit, which is not the same as being baptized with water. Most pentecostals believe that a person is baptized in the Spirit when he or she first speaks in tongues. Speaking in tongues is a strange event for people who have never seen it. The believer spontaneously begins to speak rapidly in an unknown language. There are a variety of pentecostals, and not all practice the same gifts in worship. Nonwhite pentecostals are especially active and create a lot of movement during the service. Pentecostals, like fundamentalists, preached against liberalism; but their complaint was with the formal, middle-class character of mainstream denominations. The movement is especially attractive to the poor and oppressed people of the world. Social action is not important to pentecostals because they believe that only the second coming of Christ will change society. In the meantime, it is the Christian's duty to be converted and baptized in the Spirit.

➤ Identify the following comments as stereotypes and complaints about pentecostals:

- They are crazy in worship.
- They try to force the spiritual gifts down people's throats.
- The emotions displayed in worship are just a show.
- They don't care about the real problems of the world.
- They are wild in worship and uptight the rest of the time.

➤ Ask the youth to respond to the following statements by writing "true" or "false" in the column labeled "Pentecostal"; then invite them to tally up their points:

1. I believe that speaking in tongues is the true sign that a person is a believer. (5)
2. I believe that worship should include the practice of the spiritual gifts. (4)
3. I don't like formal, quiet worship. (2)
4. I don't think anything is going to improve the world except the second coming of Christ. (3)
5. I believe that people should live a moral life until Christ comes again. (1)

Which Stairway?

➤ Tell the youth to compare their scores. Ask:

What was your highest score?

Were you surprised by your scores? Why?

Don't Box Me In

➤ Choose four volunteers to represent each category: evangelical, liberal, fundamentalist, pentecostal. (This activity could be embarrassing or threatening; choose your volunteers carefully.)

➤ Ask the person representing the evangelicals to put the cardboard box over his or her head. Invite the other members of the group to yell out stereotypes and complaints about evangelicals.

➤ Then ask the person representing the liberals to put the box on his or her head. Invite the class to shout complaints about liberals. Repeat the process for fundamentalists and pentecostals.

➤ Discuss the following questions:

How did you feel about being boxed in and labeled?

How did you feel hurling stereotypes and insults at the person in the box?

Most of us fit into all four categories. How did you feel about being confined to one category?

How do people react when somebody tries to box them in?

How do the stereotypes differ from the ways you identify yourself?

What does it mean if the stereotypes fit?

Rubber Hits the Road

➤ Have Bibles and commentaries on hand for reference.

➤ Read aloud the following scenario:

> Kyle Williams was white and thirteen years old. He attended public school. His best friend was a girl, Kenesha Miller, who was thirteen and African-American. They had been good friends since the second grade. Kyle's other friends teased him because his best friend was a girl. When he was younger, he took the teasing to heart; and for a time, he stayed away from Kenesha. Now that he was thirteen and interested in the opposite sex, Kenesha was a great friend because she could explain to him the mystery of creatures called girls. The other day in school, he ran into a problem he had never considered before. Bobby, the class bully, came up to him as he was walking down the hall with Kenesha.
>
> "Hey Williams, slumming again? Don't you know you can't date a black girl? The Bible says so," Bobby sneered with a shove.
>
> "It does not," Kyle protested, shoving him back. "Look it up."
>
> That night, Kyle did look it up and he was even more confused. He had never thought about dating Kenesha, but what if he wanted to? What did the Bible mean?

➤ Invite the class to discuss these questions and then to investigate the Scripture references that follow:

What are the main issues in the story?

Which are issues related to race? religion? social standing? teen culture?

Do you agree with Bobby that Kyle and Kenesha should "know their place"? Why? Why not?

What was Kyle's dilemma? What would you say to him?

➤ Ask the participants to form four groups; assign one of the following Scriptures to each group:

Deuteronomy 7:1-6
Jeremiah 29:1-8
Matthew 28:16-20
Matthew 10:5-15

➤ Provide commentaries for research. Invite the groups to discuss these questions:

What is the primary message of the passage?

What, according to the commentary, is the context or setting of the story?

What is a comparable setting today?

How would you interpret the Scripture if you were an evangelical? a liberal? a fundamentalist? a pentecostal?

When the Bible doesn't fit in with the values of our culture, should we throw out the whole Bible? Why? Why not? Should we change the culture's values?

If you don't want to throw out the whole Bible, how do you decide what to keep and what to toss?

Who should decide what we believe and what we should not believe?

Worship

➤ Read aloud Galatians 3:23-29.

➤ Invite the group to sing "Peace Like a River."

➤ Conclude the session with a prayer for Christian unity.

Giving unto Caesar: When Religion Meets Politics

PURPOSE: To make youth aware that many political conflicts in today's world are rooted in religious issues.

Preparation

➤ Make copies of the two inventories, "Temperature Check" and "Like I Care."

➤ Have available paper, pencils, Bibles, one or two topical concordances, and Bible commentaries.

➤ A smaller group will need large sheets of paper and felt-tip markers. A larger group will need a ballot box and slips of paper, as well as a place to debate and to hold a press conference.

Check Your Temperature

Many youth today think they don't care about politics. After all, politics is just a game that old fogies and Baby Boomers play. Still, teenagers who pretend apathy seem to be well aware of the political world. Many politicians—and many religious people—claim that religious conversation has no place in political discussions. Yet religious groups are clearly a factor in today's political climate.

"Temperature Check" will help the group focus on their political and religious interests and feelings. The activity "Like I Care" at the end of the program will help them measure shifts of interest or opinion.

➤ Distribute pencils and copies of "Temperature Check." Ask each person to complete the inventory.

➤ Then invite the group to take a break so that you can check their answers. Bring the group together to talk about the results.

TEMPERATURE CHECK

Fill in the blanks:

1. I think politics is _____

2. I think religion is _____

3. If I could have voted in the last presidential election

I would have voted for _____

Underline one answer to complete the sentence:

4. My parents (ARE) (ARE NOT) involved in politics.

5. I think politics has a (SMALL) (MEDIUM) (LARGE) influence on my life.

6. My friends care about politics (A LITTLE) (A LOT) (NOT AT ALL).

7. The Bible says (A LITTLE) (A LOT) (NOTHING) about politics.

8. Religious people (SHOULD) (SHOULD NOT) be involved in politics.

Is the statement true or false?

9. All politicians are corrupt.

Answer the question:

10. Who were two people who signed the Declaration of Independence? (Check the *World Almanac* or an encyclopedia.)

_____

_____

Battles on the Homefront

➤ Ask the group to name several issues that might be rooted in or influenced by religion.

➤ Invite the youth to read and discuss one of the following issues; have available Bibles and concordances so that the participants can find out what the Bible says about the issue they select.

Abortion
FACTS TO KNOW

■ In 1973, Roe vs. Wade made abortion legal in the United States. The Supreme Court maintained that a woman and her physician could decide to terminate a pregnancy during the first twenty weeks.

■ Many states have restricted abortion over the years. In 1989, a court decision upheld a Missouri law that prohibited public employees from performing abortions or using public buildings to perform abortions.

■ Jerry Falwell formed the conservative Moral Majority to oppose abortion rights.

■ Laws have been passed that prohibit pro-life activists from interfering with access to buildings in which abortions might be performed.

QUESTIONS TO CONSIDER
What does abortion have to do with religion?

In what ways does religion influence people's opinions about abortion?

Are all Christians against abortion?

What does *pro-life* mean?

What does *pro-choice* mean?

Should Christians be involved in the discussion about abortion? Why? Why not?

Prayer in School
FACTS TO KNOW

■ In 1962, the Supreme Court prohibited state schools from requiring students to recite a prayer during the school day, even if it was a nondenominational prayer and even if students could be excused from saying it. In response to several challenges, the Supreme Court has upheld its decision.

■ Prayer was banned in school because it was considered unfair to students who did not believe at all or who believed in a religion different from the faith of the person praying. On the other hand, the Constitution of the United States clearly supports freedom of religion and religious expression. Now many Americans feel they are being denied their constitutional rights to pray without interference.

■ Some students are responding to the restrictions with a program called Meet Me at the Pole, in which interested students gather at the school flagpole for a time of prayer before or after school.

QUESTIONS TO CONSIDER
Should prayer be a required school activity? Why? Why not?

How could prayer help or hinder public education?

What, do you think, was the intent of the Constitution in separating church and state?

Is there or should there be a difference between freedom of religious expression and religious participation in conversations about law and morality? Why? Why not?

Should all religious people be allowed to pray publicly? Should members of a cult or people who worship Satan be permitted free religious expression? Why? Why not?

In what ways would school prayer be harmful?

Sex Education
FACTS TO KNOW

■ In American schools, sex education has become more extensive. Yet the teenage pregnancy rate continues to rise.

■ The debate concerns who should be responsible for teaching kids the facts of life. Should parents, religious institutions, peers, or schools be responsible? Should teenagers find out for themselves how reproduction works?

■ Another aspect of the debate concerns the values, religious and otherwise, that are taught along with the facts of procreation.

■ Some religious groups strongly oppose sex education in schools.

QUESTIONS TO CONSIDER
Should sex education be the responsibility of schools? parents? religious groups? Who should have primary responsibility?

How did you find out about sex?

What values, if any, should be included in sex education?

Given AIDS and other sexually transmitted diseases, should education include an emphasis on abstinence? Why? Why not?

Should condoms be provided by schools?

Is sexual activity among teenagers inevitable?

What should be the church's role in sex education?

Global Warming Isn't What You Think

➤ Ask the youth to name hot spots around the world, where nations or people are involved in war or other types of conflict. Ask:

Do any of the conflicts in the world today involve religious issues?

Why are people willing to sacrifice their lives for the sake of religion?

➤ Invite the group to read "Koshko and Kalina," a hypothetical situation in which religious and political issues are at the root of a conflict that disrupts two people's lives. Ask the youth to identify the issues and to propose solutions.

Koshko and Kalina

Koshko lives in Sarajevo. He is twenty-three years old and a Bosnian Muslim. Until a few years ago, his country was called Yugoslavia; and it was behind the Iron Curtain. Under Communist rule, the people had little freedom; but they were learning to get along after centuries of fighting. Life was at least tolerable.

That was before the Iron Curtain was torn down. When the Communist regime crumbled, all the old hatreds flared up again. Over half the population of Sarajevo is Christian; about three percent of the people are Muslims. The Serbs, who are mostly Christian, decided to take over the whole country and to expel the Muslims. When the Muslims fought back, the Serbs began a campaign of cultural genocide that was designed to wipe out the Muslims forever. The United Nations imposed an embargo on arms to the region and succeeded in preventing the Bosnian Muslims from defending themselves. The Serbs had most of Yugoslavia's arms at their disposal.

Koshko was in love with Kalina. They fell in love when they were fifteen. He loved her smile, her quick wit, the way her eyes lit up when she saw him. But now everything had changed. He last saw Kalina six months ago. And when he saw her, she didn't smile; she hardly acknowledged his presence. They met on the streets of Sarajevo. Dodging sniper bullets, Koshko managed to pull Kalina into a doorway and to look into her eyes; but her eyes were clouded with grief and pain.

"Never do that again," she scolded. "You want to get us both killed? I can't see you anymore." She pulled away and ran down the street. That was the last time Koshko saw her. Kalina was Serbian. For them to be seen together would mean death for them and possibly for their families.

Competing Claims

➤ Read or paraphrase the following information:

In Israel, the issues of life and death and hope and faith come together in the fate of Jerusalem. Three major world religions—Judaism, Christianity, and Islam—claim Israel as their own and sometimes claim the same shrines. The conflict in Israel is ancient, rooted in the Torah. Centuries ago, the children of Israel were led by Moses into the Promised Land. Although the land was promised to Abraham, it was already occupied. Judaism, Christianity, and Islam all trace their heritage to Abraham and Moses. Through the ages, one group or another has been fighting for the right to claim the tiny land of Israel.

➤ Invite the youth to look at the conflict through the eyes of youth living in Jerusalem. Ask volunteers to read the parts of Leah, Hakeem, and Abraham. Then ask the group to compare and contrast the three perspectives.

■ LEAH: I am nineteen-years-old, and I am in the army. I am proud to be a Jew. Over the centuries, our people have put up with enough. We want to live in Israel, the land God promised us. We want peace; but if an Arab starts throwing rocks at me, I'm going to fire my gun. It's as simple as that.

■ HAKEEM: I'm an Arab, and I'm a Christian. I am sick of the Jews. They come in here and act like they own the place. They took away my family's land. They called it national security; I call it theft. Every day, I throw rocks at soldiers. My little brother was killed, but I will not stop fighting until my people are free.

■ ABRAHAM: I'm an Arab and a Muslim. The Qu'ran speaks of a Holy War, but it means a spiritual war. We are to defend our faith, but I feel that all the killing is wrong. I hope we can find peace somehow.

Here's What the Bible Says

➤ Arrange the chairs in a circle. Place two chairs facing each other in the center of the circle. Ask the youth to form two teams. Tell a representative from each team to sit in the center of the circle. Explain that you will ask a question; both teams will research and discuss the question by reading Scripture. Then the two people in the center of the circle will argue two opposing positions. The people on their teams should observe quietly.

➤ Allow about ten minutes for preparation and five minutes for each team's representative to state the team's position.

➤ Question: Should religious people be involved in politics? Ask the youth to read **Matthew 22:15-22** before they debate the issue.

➤ Question 2: Should a national flag be allowed in

church? Ask the youth to read **Romans 13:1-7** and **Psalm 33** before they debate the issue.

Hail to the Chief

➤ Read or paraphrase the following information:

For over two hundred years, the president of the United States has been a white male Christian; most have been Protestants. A deist or two may have sneaked into the White House early on; but the 1960 election of John Kennedy, a Roman Catholic, created a controversy.

Religion was a big issue in the 1992 election, as well as in almost every election that has gone before. Bill Clinton is a devout Baptist. He worships regularly, and he often brings his faith into discussions. But Bill Clinton is a thorn in the side of many of his Baptist brothers and sisters. He supports abortion and rights for homosexuals, and his marital fidelity has been questioned. The Southern Baptist Convention has considered a proposal to kick him out. Baptist churches are independent and make their own decisions about membership. The proposal was defeated.

➤ Be clear that "Hail to the Chief" is a discussion starter to encourage conversation about public officials and the expectations of the church. It is not intended to focus on the Southern Baptist Convention and Mr. Clinton. Ask:

Is the president's faith important to the American people? Should it be important? Why?

Why have only Christians held the office of president? Should high public office be open to people of all religious groups? Why? Why not?

Do you measure character and leadership ability by how a person worships and what he or she believes? Why? Why not?

Do you think a church has the right to kick out a public official if he or she doesn't meet the church's expectations? Does a church have the right to kick out anyone?

For a Smaller Group
➤ Ask the youth to draw on a large sheet of paper a picture of the ideal president. Then invite them to write on the picture the characteristics they think are important for a good president. Ask:

Is it important for the president to be religious?

For a Large Group
➤ Invite the group to hold a mock presidential election. They should begin by deciding who will be the candidates (at least two) and who will be the candidates' campaign managers, reporters, speech writers, spouses, children, and parents. They should also agree on who will convene the debate.

➤ Suggest that the group begin by conducting a debate, a town meeting, and a press conference. Then they should hold the election.

➤ After the election, invite the group to discuss why the candidate won. Be sure to ask if the person's religion and his or her character were factors in the election.

Do You Care?

➤ Distribute pencils and copies of the inventory "Like I Care." The inventory will help the participants measure, after the session, their interest and feelings about religion and politics.

LIKE I CARE
Is the statement true or false?

1. I don't care about politics.

2. I think religion is private and has nothing to do with politics.

3. I think religious people have a responsibility to get involved in politics.

4. I think Jesus wants us to work through political channels to make a better world.

5. I think Jesus wants us to leave the political system to rot.

6. A president should be a religious person.

7. A president should be a Christian person.

8. Religion should not be a part of discussions about political issues, such as abortion or civil rights.

9. Religion should play a role in politics.

10. Religion can and does play a role in politics.

➤ Invite the youth to review their answers and to compare them to the information gained in "Temperature Check." Then ask:

What difference does it make if religion plays a part in public conversation and decision-making?

As a person of faith, how can you bring your religious beliefs to the political arenas in which you participate, such as school elections, clubs, or community service projects?

Are public decisions that are made without regard for religious values good decisions for the people they affect? Why? Why not?

Worship

➤ Invite the group to pray the Prayer of St. Francis or another prayer for peace.

➤ Conclude the session by inviting the youth to sing "Let There Be Peace on Earth."

"Those People"

> **PURPOSE:** *To examine the nature of fears caused by religious differences in order to overcome them.*

Preparation

➤ Cut paper into small squares. Be sure you have pencils and tape. Collect plastic figurines (like plastic soldiers) to use with "The Results of Fear."

➤ Have available a Bible for each person, commentaries on **Genesis**, and a topical concordance.

Things We Do for God

➤ Summarize "Religious Mayhem" (see the box on this page). Then discuss the following questions:

What do you think about the facts of our religious history?

Why, do you think, would people commit crimes in the name of religion?

How strongly do you feel about your religion? Would you commit a crime for a religious cause? Why? Why not?

Is it good or bad to be so devout? Why?

In the last twenty years, what hate crimes have been committed in the name of religion?

Fear

➤ Distribute paper and pencils. Tell the youth to write descriptions or to draw pictures of people they would be afraid of if they met them walking down the street. What kind of person would make them cross over to the other side of the street or at least avert their eyes?

➤ Invite volunteers to show their pictures or to read their descriptions. Then discuss these questions:

What about the person you described or drew would make you afraid or nervous?

Did your fear have anything to do his or her religion?

What kind of religious person would make you cross the street to avoid him or her? Why?

Religious Mayhem

The history of the world is pockmarked with murders and mayhem committed in the name of God and religion. In the early days of the Bible, Elijah killed the priests of Ba'al to prove the might of Jehovah. Why can't we live with religious differences? Take a look at some of the religious hate crimes that mark our history:

■ The early Hebrews were enslaved by the Egyptians because they were not strong enough to resist.

■ The fledgling Christian church refused to burn incense to the Roman emperor and had to go underground to escape persecution.

■ The Romans and later the Christians invaded Britain and wiped out the tribal nature religion that once flourished there.

■ During the Crusades, Christians tried to force Jews and Muslims to convert.

■ In the name of Christian mission, white imperialists from all over the globe forced their religion and their culture on the people of Africa and both North and South Americas.

■ Adolf Hitler committed the greatest atrocities of the twentieth century against Jews, gypsies, homosexuals, the mentally ill—anyone who didn't fit the Aryan ideal. For the most part, the church remained silent as the trains rolled into the death camps.

■ Synagogues in America have experienced hate crimes: vandalism, phone calls, even arson. Jews have been attacked for wearing a yarmulke.

■ In Israel, a Jewish settler walked into a Muslim mosque and, with an automatic weapon, killed several worshipers while they were on their knees in prayer.

■ In New York City, a group of Islamic extremists set off a bomb in the World Trade center, killing and injuring several people.

■ Racial, ethnic, and religious hatred is alive and well in the United States. Hate crimes are on the rise.

➤ Read each of the descriptions listed below. After each, ask these questions:

Would you be afraid of them?

Whom would they frighten?

Why would they frighten people? In what ways is their religion frightening?

- a group of Arabs driving a van
- Israeli soldiers walking down a Jerusalem street with automatic rifles slung over their shoulders
- a group of black teenagers walking through government housing
- three middle-aged white men sitting on a front porch cradling their shotguns
- a large group of Hispanic teenagers talking loudly in Spanish
- three policemen cruising a rough neighborhood
- two elderly black women making a voodoo sign
- Asian men, maybe martial arts experts, carrying large canes
- four women dressed in leather and chains and riding motorcycles to a nightclub
- a group of skinheads
- feminists at a pro-choice rally
- Black Muslims at worship
- participants in a Ku Klux Klan parade

A Study in Fear

➤ Read aloud **Genesis 34**. Have a commentary available.

➤ Invite discussion using these questions:

Why were Dinah's brothers so angry? Was it because of Dinah's pain? because the man who raped her was of another race? Why?

Circumcision defines a Jew. It is a ritual given to the Jewish people by God and identifies them as the chosen people. When Hamor and Shechem and the others were circumcised, what did it mean?

Could the story in Genesis be understood as the ancient equivalent of a terrorist attack by a religious group? Why? Why not?

Did Hamor and Shechem intend to live at peace with Jacob and his sons?

One reason Shechem and Hamor mingled with the Jews was to benefit from their wealth. Does their economic motive remove the motives of race or religion? Why? Why not?

What other fears can you identify in this story, other than Dinah's own private terror because of the rape?

What Are People Afraid of?

➤ Say to the group: "Most people are afraid of whatever is different, whether another person's looks or actions or beliefs. Differences challenge what we believe about the world."

➤ Ask the youth to form two or three groups. Ask each group to choose one of the following activities:

■ Write a song or a poem about differences and how they are overcome. Make a videotape or an audiotape of the group's performing the song or reading the poem.

■ Write a skit or a short play about differences and how they are overcome. Make a videotape or an audiotape of the group's performing the play.

➤ Bring the groups together. Ask the members of each group to present their activity and to lead a discussion about what they learned.

The Results of Fear

➤ Give every class member at least one plastic figurine. Distribute small squares of paper, pencils, and tape.

➤ Ask the youth to write on the squares of paper the following names or descriptions and to tape one label on each figurine:

Hari Krishna	Buddhist monk
Billy Graham	Rush Limbaugh
Jewish rabbi	Ronald Reagan
Hillary Clinton	Arsenio Hall
Snoop Doggy Dog	Garth Brooks
Jimmy Swaggart	Saddam Hussein
Nelson Mandela	Bob Dole
Bill Clinton	Amy Grant
Howard Stern	Madonna

➤ Invite discussion by asking these questions:

What do you know or think you know about the religious perspective of the person assigned to you? (See the articles beginning on page 48.)

How did you find out about his or her religious perspective? Did you find out from articles in this book? from magazines, newspapers, talk shows, movies, or television news? from album covers or record promotions?

What part does religion seem to play in the person's life?

➤ Ask the participants to sit in a circle and to arrange the figurines in front of them. The youth will move the figurines toward the center of the circle when the characters represented would choose to state an opinion. (Not all the issues will be relevant to all the characters.)

➤ Invite the youth to debate these issues:

■ Should prayer or spiritual exercises of any kind be allowed in school?

■ Is it important that our personal beliefs and actions be consistent with our public beliefs and actions?

■ Under what conditions, if any, should a religious person approve of abortion?

Why Does Religion Make People Behave So Badly?

➤ Invite the participants to discuss the following scenarios:

■ You are an 18-year-old Iraqi Muslim male and have witnessed a leader from another country ordering bombs to be dropped on the Iraqi people. The leader is an infidel, a nonbeliever, and has ordered the attack because Iraq will not get rid of its leader, who is a believer. How do you react?

■ The Bible says that women should keep quiet in church. Today women are assertive and speak up for themselves. They are even pastors. You are a Christian, and you read the Bible literally. How do you react?

■ You are a 70-year-old Jew who lost both parents and a sister in the Holocaust. You have settled in Israel, the holy place, which you believe was given to your people by God. You think Palestinians and other Arabs want to drive your people into the sea and take Israel away from the Jews. How do you react?

Cures for Fears

➤ Choose one of the following activities:

■ Invite the pastor to talk about what it would be like for the church to adopt a refugee family. The family should be from Bosnia or another country that is involved in a religious war.

■ Ask a family who has sponsored an exchange student to talk to the group about what it was like. If possible, invite a family who has sponsored a student whose religion was different from their own.

■ Tell the youth to read "Joy's Story" (see the box on page 31). Then ask these questions:

What are the key events, attitudes, and beliefs mentioned in the story? Do you agree or disagree with them? Why?

Behbood, Masood, and Saieed were like strangers in a strange land. Did they have reasons to be afraid? Why? Why not?

Would living every day with a person of another culture or religion reduce fear? Why? Why not?

What fears would the Iranian brothers have had?

What fears would the sponsoring family have had?

How would you have felt, thought, and acted if you had been a member of the American family? of the Iranian family?

In America, people from various religious and cultural backgrounds talk to one another, live in the same neighborhoods, go to school together. Why are people still prejudiced?

Worship

➤ Select one of the youth to lead the litany. After he or she reads each section of the litany, the group will respond, saying, "I will not be afraid."

Leader: I am a Christian living in a Muslim country.
Group: I will not be afraid.
Leader: I am a Sikh, but I live surrounded by Hindus and Muslims.
Leader: I am a Jew living in Israel with Arab Muslims and Christians.
Leader: I am an Arab Muslim living in America.
Leader: I am a Buddhist. I go to public school in Des Moines, Iowa.
Leader: I am a Hindu living in America. It's hard to practice my faith in such a strange country.
Leader: I am the Lord your God who loves all people. I tell you, do not be afraid.

➤ Conclude the session by inviting the group to sing "We Shall Overcome."

Joy's Story

When I was a child, I was never sure how many brothers and sisters I had because my family was always adopting foreign students and their families. I remember Anschalee from Thailand, Masood and his family from Iran, Salem from the Arab Emirates, Benny from Germany, and countless others whose names I don't remember.

Masood Orangi and his family were the most important. Masood came to the United States from Iran in order to study engineering at the University of Louisville. My family adopted him through a program in our church. I was eleven; and Masood, the oldest in a family of seven, was well-versed in the art of big brothering.

I guess you know that Iran is an Islamic country. The women in Iran have their heads covered when they go out in public. Whenever people drive from place to place, no matter how hurried they are, they stop at every alms box and toss in some cash. And almost everyone stops whatever they are doing to pray five times a day.

It wasn't long before Masood's younger brother Behbood came to the United States as well. He was not quite finished with high school, so he lived with us for awhile and went to our school. Behbood was a delightful person with an easy smile and ready wit. He was easy to love as a brother.

However, my own brothers and I were not especially nice to Behbood. For a while, we had him convinced that his destiny on earth was to be the garbage man for the household. With stealth and cunning and behind Mom's back, we told him he had to take out the garbage every day. We even took to calling him garbage man. He got wise before long; and one night when we told him to take out the garbage, he said with a sly grin, "Mom said you to do it."

Little brother Saieed was the next to come over. He had a ways to go before he finished high school, so he lived with us the longest. Saieed was not as easy to get along with as his brother Behbood. But through the rocky times, we learned to love even Saieed.

When I was in the seventh grade, I wrote a paper on Islam. I interviewed Masood. When I found out that Muslims believe that Jesus was a great prophet, but not the Son of God, I was scandalized. But learning about another religion didn't hurt me; I'm still hangin' with the United Methodists.

Masood went back to Iran so that he could go into business with his father. Behbood married an American girl and lives in Lexington, Kentucky, with her and their two kids. Saieed hasn't married yet. He's a professor in Ohio, and I'm sure he's tormenting his students. We still keep in touch. They are still my brothers, and I guess they always will be.

Who Is My Neighbor?

> **PURPOSE: To help the youth learn to be citizens in the global village with hospitality and without prejudice.**

Preparation

➤ Have available nametags, pens, and felt-tip markers and large sheets of paper or chalk and a chalkboard. Provide Bibles and commentaries on the **Gospel of Luke.**

➤ Many denominations require an ordained person to consecrate Communion elements. Check with your pastor. If he or she is unavailable, use the alternative worship service.

The Question

➤ Tell the youth to read **Luke 10:25-29**. (The group will study the story of the good Samaritan one section at a time. Be sure they don't read more than the designated verses.)

➤ Say to the class: "Apparently the young man who came to Jesus wanted to cover all his bases and make sure that he would do all the right things to get into heaven. The problem was that he didn't want to do any more than the minimum requirements. (Sort of like a teenager who obeys his mother's request to take out the garbage, but as he stuffs the garbage in the can, conveniently ignores the trash that the dogs have spread all over the lawn.) The young man in the Scripture, wanting to avoid the hard work of loving neighbors, asked, 'Who is my neighbor?' Jesus' answer turned out to be a real zinger."

➤ Discuss these questions:

Did the young man want to please Jesus or himself?

Did he care about his neighbor?

How do you imagine Jesus would answer?

Who is your neighbor?

Who is not your neighbor? Who can take care of himself or herself in a time of trouble?

Good Guy; Bad Luck

➤ Tell the group to read **Luke 10:30.**

➤ Set the stage by saying, "The road between Jerusalem and Jericho was notorious. It snaked through the wilderness; for a good part of a traveler's journey, the view from the road was nothing but rocks, sand, and more rocks. The road was lined with steep rocky cliffs: the perfect place for a thief to hide. Travelers on the road got mugged all the time. There was nothing unusual about the poor guy's fate. He was, in all likelihood, a good Jew walking to Jericho on business, minding his own business. The thieves showed him no mercy. They didn't just take his wallet; they stripped him of his clothes, beat him senseless, and left him for dead. He was not a pretty sight, lying there in the ditch."

➤ Discuss the fact that bad things happen to good people:

Did the traveler deserve to be beaten?

How could he have avoided it?

Do bad things happen to good people?

➤ Invite the youth to name good people who have had bad things happen to them.

The Other Side

➤ Ask the group to read **Luke 10:31-32.**

➤ Say to the class: "A priest was a member of the Jewish clergy, and a Levite was a Temple assistant. The parable doesn't say why the priest and the Levite didn't stop. Scholars have suggested reasons: A good Jew was forbidden to touch a dead body, and the victim looked like he was no longer among the living. If the priest and the Levite had touched him on their way to the Temple, they would have had to go home and purify themselves again. Another reason could have been fear. A common ploy among thieves was to send someone to the ditch to pretend to be hurt so that somebody else would stop and offer assistance. Then the other thieves would run out and nail him."

➤ Talk over these questions:

How do you feel about the priest and the Levite?

Would they have put themselves at risk if they had stopped?

Do you stop for hitchhikers? Why? Why not?

A few years ago, a man was murdered by people he stopped to help on the highway. How did his murder affect other travelers?

Would you have stopped to help the guy in the ditch?

➤ Encourage the youth to choose one of the following optional activities to further illustrate the story:

THE DAVID BETTERMAN SHOW

Select two or three people to play the part of David Betterman and to create a list of the ten best reasons to avoid helping an injured traveler. Then invite them to take turns reading the reasons aloud. Invite the audience to challenge any or all of David Betterman's reasons and to come up with a new list of the ten best reasons to help the injured traveler. Be sure the youth keep in mind all the characters in the story.

THE TRIAL

Roleplay a trial. The characters should include a judge, a prosecutor, a defense attorney, and members of the jury. The traveler, the thieves, the priest, and the Levite are on trial to defend their actions. The jury must decide if and how they should have acted differently.

Heroes

➤ Ask a volunteer to read aloud **Luke 10:33.**

➤ Say to the group: "The hero arrived, just like we knew he would. Jesus' audience was expecting a hero too. They had heard other versions of the story: A man fell victim to thieves; the clergy and the lawyers were too good to touch him. But along came an ordinary good Jew, who helped him out. Don't you love hero stories?"

➤ Ask the class to consider the question:

Who are your heroes?

➤ Write the groups' answers on the chalkboard or on a large sheet of paper.

➤ Read the list of heroes below. Ask these questions about each one:

What makes him or her a hero?

If you met him or her in a dark alley, would you be relieved or afraid?

■ Batman
■ Jesus
■ Mother Teresa
■ Michael Landon
■ Jackie Joiner
■ Teenage Mutant Ninja Turtles
■ Maya Angelou
■ Superman
■ Amy Grant

➤ Invite the class to compose a story about a hero, a teenager who does something great for somebody else.

A What?

➤ Read aloud **Luke 10:33-35.**

➤ Say to the group: "Hold it. Something is wrong with the story. The hero isn't supposed to be a Samaritan. Jesus' audience would have been horrified at the twist in the story. The hero was supposed to be a good Jew, not a Samaritan. Jews and Samaritans were enemies. They hated each other. Jews considered Samaritans to be sneaky, lowlife losers. Samaritans considered Jews to be self-righteous. The hero in the story was not supposed to be a Samaritan."

➤ Ask the group to make a list of enemies: people or groups of people who hate each other. Write the list on the chalkboard or on a large sheet of paper.

➤ Then ask the youth to complete this story by answering the questions that follow:

■ You are riding your motorcycle down a deserted country road. You are driving too fast, of course; but it feels great. The wind is in your hair, the sun is beaming down on your back. You don't have a care in the world. That is, until your bike hits a patch of loose gravel and you go into a skid. You end up in the ditch.

How will you get help?

As you are lying there in the ditch, whose faces would you rather *not* see peering over the side of the ditch? Why?

Whom would you prefer not to see if you were an African-American male teenager? a white female teenager? a Bosnian Muslim? an Irish Catholic? a Jew from the United States? a Haitian refugee? a Hispanic migrant worker?

➤ Ask the youth to complete the story by saying that the person they would prefer not to see peers at them over the side of the ditch. Ask:

How is the hero in this story different from Batman, Superman, and the people you listed as heroes?

In the parable, would a Jew want to meet a Samaritan in a dark alley? Why? Why not?

Neighbor This!

➤ Ask the group to name ways, both civilized and not-so-civilized, in which people who hate one another avoid and hurt one another. How do people whose religion or ideologies differ treat one another? Write the groups' responses on a chalkboard or on large sheets of paper.

➤ Say to the class: "In the comics, Dagwood Bumstead and his neighbor Herb have a friendly war. Dagwood borrows Herb's tools and forgets to return them. Dagwood is in a carpool with Herb, but he is late almost every morning and makes everybody else late. Dagwood and Herb work it out, and everybody laughs in the end."

➤ Ask the youth to consider what conflicts would occur between the following people and how they might work them out:

■ two students in your school, one a Jehovah's Witness, the other a Mormon;

■ the son of a devout Catholic who wants to date the daughter of a devout member of the Church of Christ;

■ you and a person who belongs to a religious group that is generally scorned or misunderstood by your family;

In the Ditch

➤ Say to the group: "Now you are really in a bind. You're lying half dead in a ditch and the only person to come along in two hours is your mortal enemy. Your enemy is the only person who can help you."

➤ Discuss these questions:

How do you feel about letting your enemy help you?

Do you accept help?

Do you have a choice?

How does accepting help change the way you feel about your enemy?

➤ Ask the youth to consider each of the following scenarios in light of the story of the good Samaritan; encourage them to think about what God would want in each situation:

■ Elyssa's parents have been fighting for three days about her mother's participation in what her father calls a cult. Her father says he is leaving, and he wants Elyssa to come with him.

■ Ben avoids Jeremy because Jeremy keeps asking Ben to come to church. After school, Ben wrecks his car and injures himself in the accident. Jeremy is the only person who walks by.

■ Erin is looking at Catholic University because the program is especially good in her area of interest, but she doesn't want to be around a lot of people who aren't Protestant.

■ Ho Lee does very well in school. He is disciplined, motivated, and a devout Buddhist. Brian hates him and is making plans.

■ Nikki doesn't want to continue to attend her church because the congregation uses no musical instruments in worship. She wants to try out the Pentecostal church, where her friend Carmen is a member, because the service includes lively instrumental music. Her parents object.

■ John hates Jews. He thinks they are Christ-killers and greedy and sleazy. John belongs to a neo-Nazi group.

Photo by Jean-Claude LeJeune

Is My Pastor Also My Neighbor?

➤ Tell the group: "A few years ago in a small town in Indiana, the Catholic Archabbey assigned a priest to serve a church. Most of the people in the county were Roman Catholics who relied heavily on the spiritual direction provided by the priests. There was just one problem: The priest was black. The people of the all-white congregation were not at all happy. They protested, but the reply from the Archabbot was simple: 'If you are going to receive Communion, you will receive it from the hands of a black priest.' "

➤ Discuss the following questions:

Should the people have been upset about the appointment of a black priest to their parish? If the clergy appointed to your church were of a race different from the congregation's, would it create a problem? Why? Why not?

Should Christians be able to choose who will give them Communion? Why? Why not?

Did the congregation's prejudice mar the holiness of the Communion ritual? Why? Why not?

How is the story of the priest in Indiana like the story of the Good Samaritan?

Worship

➤ Write on nametags the names of people or groups of people who are enemies. Include religious and political enemies. Invite the youth to wear the nametags.

➤ Celebrate Communion or a fellowship meal using the ritual of your church. Instruct the youth to serve one another.

➤ During Communion, invite the participants to sing "Dona Nobis Pacem" or another hymn of peace and unity.

ALTERNATIVE WORSHIP

➤ Prepare nametags.

➤ Ask the youth to sit in a circle. Ask each person "Who is your neighbor?" He or she will assume the character of the person or group described on his or her nametag and will answer by naming an enemy.

➤ Invite the group to sing "Dona Nobis Pacem" or another hymn of peace and unity.

Difference Doesn't Look Alike

PURPOSE: To introduce various religions to youth and to help them develop tolerance of diversity in God's plan for the world's faith.

Preparation

➤ Have available a chalkboard and chalk or large sheets of paper and felt-tip markers for keeping score in "Cosmic Jeopardy." Have available art supplies for making a collage during worship.

➤ Check your community or church library for books of symbols or works of art that identify or typify a variety of religions.

➤ Write the closing prayer on a large sheet of paper.

➤ Have available Bibles for everyone and a commentary on **John.**

Benomi

➤ Invite the participants to read the following story:

Benomi was a Hasidic Jew. He was ultra-orthodox. He attended a Hebrew school where, in addition to English, Math, Science, and Social Studies, he studied the Torah and Mishnah and the other writings of his faith. He had a lot of friends, and they made jokes about their teachers and parents and other friends. In a lot of ways, he was an average American teenager, but in other ways he was not.

Benomi's faith taught that men should dress as they did in the nineteenth century, with black hats and long black overcoats. He wore his hair cut very short, except for the curled earlocks, which he kept long over his ears. He was growing a beard, which would someday be bushy. He did not look like an average MTV-generation kid, and he didn't care.

Benomi did not date. He lived in a neighborhood in New York City with other Hasidic Jews. He knew a lot of girls, but he was not allowed to touch them or come near them. The men and the women kept themselves separate from each other. They sat in separate parts of the temple during worship. At weddings, the men danced in one group while the women danced in another. When the people traveled together, they rode in a large bus or a van; and if men and women traveled together, a curtain divided them.

Young girls wore nothing on their heads; but when a woman was married, she wore a scarf or wig to cover her head. This was a sign that she was available to her husband only. A woman expected to be pregnant young and often and to make a career of keeping a good Jewish home for her family.

Benomi knew he would be married someday. A bride would be offered to him, and he could say yes or no to the offer. Marriages were arranged, but not without the consent of the young people who were getting married.

Benomi's life was structured and orderly. He knew pretty much what was going to happen every day of his life. He would study, and he would work, and he would not even wonder if he was happy. The goal of a Jew was not to be happy, but to be faithful to God and to the community. And yet, even with all the structure and the laws and the rules, Benomi was content. He knew he was loved.

➤ Invite discussion of the story using these questions:

What do you think of Benomi's life? Why?

Would you be comfortable with the rules and the dress code of the Hasidic community? How do you imagine Benomi felt about them?

Why were the rules important to the community?

Why is it important to understand why some religious groups choose to live differently from the rest of society?

Why should you care about Benomi's religion? What difference does it make?

Would you want him to understand and appreciate your religion? Why? Why not?

Cosmic Jeopardy

➤ Divide the group into teams of no more than five people. Choose one person to play the master of ceremonies and another person to judge and keep score. Tell each team to choose a captain; provide the captain with a bell or a whistle.

➤ The master of ceremonies will read the answer to a question. The first team to signal will attempt to state the question. If the team members answer correctly, they will receive two points. If their response is not in the form of a question, they will lose one of the points. If they answer incorrectly, another team may try to answer.

➤ Each answer read by the master of ceremonies will be a description of a world religion or a denomination. The teams must respond with a question: What is (*a world religion*)? or Who are (*the people of a Christian denomination*)?

Part 1: World Religions

1. *Answer:* The first religion to believe that God is one God.
   Question: What is Judaism? (See pages 53-56.)

2. *Answer:* A religion that grew out of Judaism and accepts the belief that the Messiah has come.
   Question: What is Christianity? (See pages 57-60.)

3. *Answer:* A religion that was born of a revelation given to the prophet Muhammad by the angel Gabriel.
   Question: What is Islam? (See pages 61-64.)

4. *Answer:* A religion that serves several gods who come from All Reality called Brahman. The gods include Brahma, Vishnu, Shiva, and the goddess Devi.
   Question: What is Hinduism? (See pages 65-68.)

5. *Answer:* A religion with no personal god, but an Enlightened One, who shared his insights with others so that they could become enlightened. The ultimate goal is Nirvana.
   Question: What is Buddhism? (See pages 69-73.)

Part 2: Christian Denominations

6. *Answer:* A family of churches that believes that people and congregations are free to make their own decisions. They practice believer's baptism. The original members of this group were called Anabaptists.
   Question: Who are Baptists? (See pages 93-95.)

7. *Answer:* A family of believers who have faith in the power of the Holy Spirit. A person who has been baptized will exhibit one or more of the spiritual gifts, including prophecy, speaking in tongues, healing, miracles.
   Question: Who are Pentecostals? (See pages 99-100.)

8. *Answer:* A family of churches that trace their heritage to John Calvin, one of the leaders of the Protestant Reformation. They believe in the sovereignty of God, that God is ultimately in control of the world, both the social order and individual lives.
   Question: Who are Presbyterians? (See pages 82-85.)

9. *Answer:* A church that was founded on the work and beliefs of Martin Luther, a German monk who nailed ninety-five of his essays on the door of a church and was branded a heretic. This group places emphasis on Scripture and creeds, as well as justification by faith alone.
   Question: Who are Lutherans? (See pages 80-81.)

10. *Answer:* A religion that was started when John Smith had a vision. Believers have their own sacred text in addition to a revised version of the Bible. The full name of the religion is The Church of Jesus Christ of Latter Day Saints.
    Question: Who are Mormons? (See pages 102-103.)

11. *Answer:* A church in the East that split from the Roman Catholic Church in 1050 C.E. It promotes unity through common beliefs and scorns the development of new denominations.
    Question: What is the Eastern Orthodox Church? (See pages 74-78.)

12. *Answer:* A church formed in 1961 from four churches that developed on the American frontier. It blends many theological traditions, but accepts the authority of Scripture, justification by faith alone, and freedom of worship. Each congregation is free to worship in the way it chooses.
    Question: What is the United Church of Christ? (See pages 82-84.)

13. *Answer:* A church founded by John Wesley, a member of the Church of England who never intended to start a new religion. Early American founders include Philip Otterbein and Jacob Albright. The beliefs of the church's members are diverse. They accept four sources of authority in matters of faith and practice: Scripture, tradition, reason, and experience.
    Question: Who are United Methodists? (See pages 90-92.)

14. (For 6 points, 2 for each church)
    Answer: Three churches that were founded by Thomas and Alexander Campbell and Barton Stone and that developed on the American frontier. They offer Communion every Sunday. In this century, the three denominations split over issues such as allowing musical instruments in church and accepting methods of baptism other than immersion.
    Question: What are the Christian Church (Disciples of Christ), the Church of Christ, and the independent Christian Churches? (See pages 97-98.)

15. *Answer:* A church that stands together, even though its membership spans the globe. It defines itself as the original, undivided church and believes that the

church is unified through its government. The seat of power for the church is located in Rome, and the highest office is held by the Pope.

Question: What is the Roman Catholic Church? (See pages 74-78.)

16. *Answer:* An American church connected to the Church of England. It offers Communion every Sunday, and its form of worship is similar to that of the Roman Catholic Church.
Question: What is the Episcopal Church? (See pages 86-88.)

➤ After the game, discuss these questions:

What is the value of knowing about religions or denominations that are different from your own?

If a person believes in God, does it matter if he or she is a member of one denomination or another? Why? Why not?

Breaking the Rules for Goodness' Sake

➤ Invite the teens to read **John 4:1-42**, then ask:

In what ways is the woman in the story different from Jesus? How are the other people in the story different from Jesus?

What does the passage say about tolerating and valuing people who are not like you?

What does it say about tolerating the religious beliefs of other people?

Is God a Christian? Is God the same god in all religions that worship a god? Why? Why not?

Can Old Time Religion Reach the 'Hood?

➤ Ask two volunteers to present the following interview. One will play the part of the interviewer and the other the part of Michael. Michael was fifteen-years-old at the time of the interview.

INTERVIEWER: How would you define old time religion?

MICHAEL: I would say it is a lot of screaming and hollering about things that don't matter in today's world.

INTERVIEWER: What do you think about old time religion?

MICHAEL: The Bible will never be outdated, but old time religion is. Jumping up and crying in church and preachers' screaming and yelling doesn't work anymore. It's lost touch with reality.

INTERVIEW: What do you mean?

MICHAEL: Talking about old stuff: Religious people talk about the Bible, but don't apply it to today. They don't think about what's going on today.

INTERVIEW: What's going on today that old time religion doesn't address?

MICHAEL: Violence, sexual diseases, education problems, death for teenagers. Lots of teenagers don't know if they will live to see tomorrow. Old time religious people don't see or realize or understand what's going on today. They are stuck in the old days. The closest they get to reality is watching the news.

INTERVIEWER: What kind of religion can reach you?

MICHAEL: Reality-involved. The Bible should be taught, but today's subjects should also be talked about. Old timers don't talk about what's going on today, just stuff that happened thousands of years ago. There are things wrong and stuff that needs to be changed.

INTERVIEWER: How many different religions are represented by students in your school?

MICHAEL: Christians, devil worshipers, Buddhists, Hindus, Muslims. Lots of different religions.

INTERVIEWER: Why should you care about somebody else's religion?

MICHAEL: Because there is stuff to be learned from everyone's religion. Who's to say who is completely right or wrong? Every religion is not the same; but just because one is not like the other, does that make it wrong?

INTERVIEWER: What needs to happen in your church?

MICHAEL: More teens preaching and teaching. We are the ones who are in touch. We have to deal with it every day. If we had a chance to speak out more, people would hear what we have to say. They hear it on the news, but reporters say what they are told. If people want the true story about teens, they need to come to us, not principals or guidance counselors. They're not teenagers. They don't know. They need to come to us.

INTERVIEWER: Do you think the Bible can speak to your life?

MICHAEL: Not really. It's thousands of years old. They didn't have bombs and guns and AIDS and crack.

INTERVIEWER: What would you like to say to religious people to help them understand?

MICHAEL: Everything is not like on TV or on the news. I go to a violent high school. There are guns and drugs. Somebody's got stuff every day. At school, if I told somebody in first period that I wanted a gun or drugs, I could have it by third period. The news tones down everything that happens; makes everything seem like a one-shot incident.

INTERVIEW: What can religion do to help the situation?

MICHAEL: A lot if it gets involved. It wants to deal with the Bible and old stuff and God. People shouldn't forget God, but they should open their eyes to what's going on now. In private schools that have Bible study in school, it helps. If Bible study was in school, kids would hear; what God wanted would be put on their conscience.

INTERVIEWER: Do you think there should be prayer in school?

MICHAEL: Yes.

INTERVIEWER: Whose prayer?

MICHAEL: Anybody that wants to pray. I've got a little story with that. When I went to another high school my freshman year, I was on the varsity football team. Our coach believed in prayer. We prayed before every game. Some parents saw it, and some kids that went to the school told their parents. And the parents came to school to have it stopped. Our football team got in trouble for praying. We had a school meeting, and the players talked. We announced to the school that what we do is because we want to thank God that we are there and to ask God to take care of us and keep us from getting hurt. We weren't forcing it on anybody. We would take the suspensions, but it's not going to stop us from praying. We kept praying, and we didn't get suspended. The administration voted for us not to pray because it was against other student's rights. The coach said he wanted us to do what God wanted us to do instead of the administration. If the situation came up again, I would do the same thing.

➤ Invite discussion using these questions:

What do you think of Michael's beliefs about old time religion? Why?

What kind of religion would reach you?

Should people who aren't Christians be allowed to pray in school?

Photo by Cleo Photography.

Do you think religious people are all out of touch? Is religion out of touch, or do religious people forget to apply their faith to life?

In what ways does faith help us live our lives?

Does learning about other religions strengthen or weaken our faith? Why?

Worship

➤ Invite the youth to look through books of symbols and art to find pictures that represent the world religions and the Christian denominations. Ask them to draw or write descriptions of the pictures to create a collage depicting the diversity of faith in God's world. Be sure all the religions are represented as equally valid.

➤ Invite the group to pray together:

God of every nation: You have brought us to this place to worship you. You have made us who we are. We worship you and we praise you for making us Christians so that we may know the light of your saving grace.

We see your grace working through many other religions. Your light shines through many doors; your music resounds across the globe. We thank you for Christ, and we see your face in our brothers and sisters around the world, who worship in other ways. Teach us to love one another. Amen.

➤ Ask the participants to join you in singing "Kum Ba Yah" or another hymn about unity in God.

Somebody Save Me from Myself

PURPOSE: To examine the notions of sin and grace in five religious traditions.

Preparation

➤ Have available large sheets of paper and felt-tip markers or a chalkboard and chalk. Provide a Bible for each participant and commentaries on **Exodus** and **Genesis.** If possible, borrow a copy of the Qu'ran from your community library.

➤ Mark in this book the articles on Christianity, Judaism, Islam, Hinduism, and Buddhism so that you can refer to them easily.

What Do You Mean by Sin?

➤ Invite the youth to examine what sin means in each of the following traditions: Judaism, Christianity, Islam, Hinduism, and Buddhism. For each religion, they should review the information in the box on page 41, read and research the Scripture, and do the exercise.

JUDAISM

➤ Ask a volunteer to read aloud **Exodus 20:1-17.**

➤ Invite the youth to play Moses Rules. Tell the youth to form ten groups (In a small class, have the participants form five groups.) Assign each group a commandment. Give the groups five minutes to talk about why their commandments are important.

➤ Bring the groups together. Ask the members of each group to defend the importance of the commandment they were assigned. After each one, allow five minutes for debate. Then ask the youth to write on the chalkboard or on a large sheet of paper the commandments in the order of their importance.

CHRISTIANITY

➤ Ask the youth to name what they think Christians consider sins. Write their answers on the chalkboard or on large sheets of paper.

➤ Invite the group to rank the sins, beginning with what

they consider to be the worst sin. Then discuss these questions:

>   Which of the sins are about separation from God?

>   Which are about our not being the people God intended us to be?

➤ Read aloud **Genesis 3.** Invite discussion using these questions:

>   What was the big sin in the story?

>   What was the result?

>   How did the sin change the relationship between God and Adam and Eve?

>   How did separation from God change the lives of Adam and Eve?

ISLAM

➤ Discuss these questions:

>   What do you think of the rules Muslims must follow?

>   How are they different from the Ten Commandments?

>   Why are right belief and following the rules so important to Muslims?

>   How would it change your life if you were required to prostrate yourself in prayer five times a day? Would you be more connected to God than you are now? Why? Why not?

>   How would your life change if you had to memorize the scriptures and prayers that even a Muslim child can recite?

HINDUISM AND BUDDHISM

➤ Invite the youth to play Good Karma-Bad Karma. Ask them to decide what actions will produce a bad karma, and tell them to rate each action from 1 to 10 according to how bad it is (10 is the worst). Write on slips of paper brief descriptions of the actions and their point values. Put the slips of paper into a bowl.

➤ Ask the group to decide what actions will produce a good karma and will ultimately release a person from the wheel of rebirth. Then tell them to rate each action from 1 to 10 according to how good it is; 10 is the best. Write on slips of paper descriptions of the actions and their point values. Put the slips of paper in another bowl.

➤ Write on a chalkboard or on large sheets of paper each person's name. Write under his or her name "good karma" and "bad karma."

➤ Pass around the bowl that contains slips of paper describing bad-karma actions. Tell each person to take a slip of paper and to read aloud the description and the point value. Record each person's points. Then pass around the bowl that contains descriptions of actions that result in good karma. Have each person draw a slip of paper and read aloud the description and point value. Record each person's points.

➤ Subtract each person's good-karma points from his or her bad-karma points. Whoever scores zero or less may escape the wheel of rebirth to be united with Ultimate Reality. Or he or she may choose to give up his or her freedom in order to help another person. The person he or she helps will remove two points from his or her score. The person who helps will be declared an Enlightened One.

Wonders to Behold

Grace is in some form in all religions, although in the religions of Asia, it is not called salvation. Grace is an elusive word that means something like dancing with God. The information in the box on page 42 summarizes what people of several religious groups believe about grace.

➤ Post a large sheet of paper and have available felt-tip markers.

JUDAISM

➤ Read aloud **Exodus 3:1-15**. Say: "The Exodus made the Jews feel like a nation of people. God's grace came to them in a powerful way: God liberated the people from slavery."

➤ Ask these questions:

Why did God choose Moses to be a central character in God's incredible act of salvation?

This is the first time God mentions God's name; what does "I Am Who I Am" mean?

Why did God choose to reveal God's name?

➤ Ask a member of the group to read aloud one or both of the prayers from the Passover service (see the box on page 42).

➤ Invite the youth to draw on a large sheet of paper

Sin in Many Languages

Judaism

For a Jew, the greatest sin is to violate the Torah, the first five books of the Hebrew Bible, in which God gave the law to the people. The Ten Commandments are a major part of the law, but there are many other laws as well. God gave the law as a special gift to the chosen people; to violate it is to defy God.

Christianity

Jews start with the gift of the Torah. Christians start there too, but assume that because of sin no one can keep the law of God. Sin for Christians means separation from God. The Apostle Paul describes sin as human beings' inability to accept their status as God's creatures, who are dependent on the Creator.

Islam

For Muslims, sin is disobedience and pride. Muslims accept that God gave God's people the gift of the law and the gift of Jesus, the prophet; but they understand the Qu'ran as God's final and most complete revelation. The Qu'ran includes specific rules about how to live: People must believe in Allah, pray facing Mecca five times a day, give alms to the poor, fast for the month of Ramadan, and make a pilgrimage to Mecca some time in their lives. The Qu'ran also specifies how Muslims will dress and what they will eat. To disobey the laws is to be an infidel, an unbeliever, which is the worst kind of sin.

Buddhism and Hinduism

Sin and salvation are foreign to the religions of southern Asia: Hinduism and Buddhism. They do not ask the same questions that Jews, Christians, and Muslims ask. But they believe in karma, which follows a person from life to life and keeps him or her in the wheel of rebirth. Karma is the total effect or consequence of a person's actions or works, and it determines his or her destiny. Karma means that people create their own fate. The equivalent of sin in Hinduism is to do evil, to thwart the traditional ways of life, to become caught up in this world rather than in devotion to god. For a Buddhist, sin would be the opposite of the eightfold path: wrong beliefs, wrong morality, wrong meditation.

The Wonder of Grace

Judaism

Grace for Jews comes from following the laws of God. God gave the law to Moses, who brought it to the chosen people.

The Jews have a holy day called Yom Kippur, which means the Day of Atonement. It is a time for confessing sins, making amends for wrongdoing, and seeking forgiveness. A ram's horn, the shofar, is sounded at the end of Yom Kippur.

These are prayers from the Passover service, which celebrates the Exodus:

"This is the bread of affliction which Israel ate in the land of Egypt. It is a symbol of days of slavery and pain, endured by the Jewish people for centuries. It is a symbol also of the slavery and pain of so many in the world today. It is our hope that next year we will be free, that next year humankind will be free of all oppressions . . . Let all who are hungry for bread and freedom come to partake, to celebrate, the bread and freedom of this Passover celebration.

"Blessed are you, Lord our God, Ruler of the Universe who brings forth bread from the earth . . . Blessed are you, Lord our God, Ruler of the universe who sanctified us with your commandments and commanded us to eat of matza."

(from *The Passover Celebration*; Liturgy Training Publications, Archdiocese of Chicago, 1980.)

Christianity

Christians understand grace as God's love given to us even though we don't deserve it. God's grace is given in the death and resurrection of Jesus Christ and in word and sacrament.

Roman Catholics have a sacrament called Penance. They must confess their sins to a priest before they are ready to receive Communion.

Many churches include in their worship services a prayer of confession, which is prayed in unison. The pastor declares that in Jesus Christ we are forgiven.

For some Christians, going to the altar for prayer during worship is a way to confess sins and to receive forgiveness.

In our culture, even counseling can be a way of receiving grace. Many people feel more comfortable talking about their sins with their pastor or with a trained counselor, rather than saying formal prayers of confession..

Islam

For a Muslim, grace means submission to the will of Allah (God). The goal of life is not happiness, but faithfulness to God. The Qur'an tells a good Muslim how to be faithful.

Five times a day, Muslims stop whatever they are doing and pray. They may pray alone, with their families, or with a group in public. Prayers are recited in Arabic and according to a particular ritual:

1. Preparation for prayer includes washing hands, face, and feet with water or clean sand; spreading a prayer rug; removing shoes; covering the head.
2. Muslims pray facing the holy city of Mecca.
3. They begin by touching their earlobes, and saying "Allah akbar," which means "God is great."
4. Then they drop their hands to just below their waist and continue to pray. The most common prayer is the first part of the Qur'an:

In the name of Allah, the merciful, the
  compassionate.
Praise be to Allah, the Lord of the Worlds,
The merciful, the compassionate, the ruler of the
  Judgment Day!
Thee we serve and Thee we ask for aid,
Guide us in the right path,
The path of those to whom Thou art gracious;
Not of those with whom Thou art wroth;
Nor of those who err.

5. Muslims bend at the waist, put their hands on their knees, and say, "Glory to the Almighty."
6. Then they stand and say "May God accept the word of His praiser."
7. They bow in humility before Allah. Prostrate, so that their knees and toes are on the ground, their arms and hands outstretched, and their forehead touching a prayer stone or the ground, they say "Glory be to God!"
8. They sit with legs crossed and say "Allah Akbar."
9. Finally, prostrate again, they repeat the words, "Glory be to God. Allah Akbar."

Hinduism and Buddhism

The goal for a Hindu is to escape the wheel of rebirth and to be united with Ultimate Reality. Reincarnation is punishment; to escape is to overcome the grip of karma by reaching perfection in the final state of moksha. The goal for a Buddhist is to end the pattern of rebirth and to reach Nirvana, which is a state of peace and enlightenment. A person can reach Nirvana in this life, as the Buddha did. To reach the goal, to conquer the desire and cravings for pleasure, the Buddhist follows an eightfold path, which includes right understanding, thought, speech, action, work, effort, mindfulness, and concentration.

symbols that represent God's grace for the Jews. They might include scrolls, the tablets of the ten commandments, a prayer shawl, the burning bush, and so on.

CHRISTIANITY

➤ Ask the class:

How do Christians understand grace?

How do Christians receive God's grace?

➤ Invite the class to talk about how the sacraments of baptism and Communion are avenues of God's grace.

➤ Then invite the youth to consider each of the forms of confession discussed in the box on page 42.

➤ Say to the class: "Traditionally, we confess our sins during the season of Lent." Then ask the class to talk about Lent: What is it? When is it? How is it celebrated? Why is it celebrated?

➤ Then say: "Even though Christmas is a wonderful holiday, it is not the holiest day for Christians." Ask the class to discuss the meaning of Easter: What happened on Easter? Why is it important?

➤ Invite the class to draw, on the same large sheet of paper, symbols that represent grace for Christians. They may draw a cross, a fish, a butterfly, bread, wine, water.

ISLAM

➤ Invite the youth to read about what grace means for Muslims.

➤ Then say: "Every day, five times a day, a Muslim prays from memory a variety of prayers and scriptures." Ask volunteers to try out the form of prayer described in the box on page 42.

➤ Invite the group to draw on the large sheet of paper symbols that represent grace for Muslims. They may draw pictures of the Qu'ran, Mecca, a prayer rug, an alms box, or they may write the word Allah.

HINDUISM AND BUDDHISM

➤ Invite the group to discuss each one of the eight steps on the path to enlightenment (see the box on page 42 and the article on Buddhism). Ask these questions:

Why is each step included in the path to enlightenment?

Would it be hard to follow the eightfold path? Which part would be most difficult? Why?

When you think of reincarnation, do you think of it as a punishment? Would Hindus and Buddhists understand it as punishment? Why? Why not?

➤ Invite the group to draw on the large sheet of paper symbols or pictures of grace for Hindus and Buddhists. The symbols may include release from the wheel of rebirth, prayer, meditation, an eightfold path.

How Should a Person Live?

➤ Post five large sheets of paper. Draw on each an outline of a person. Write one of the following at the top of each sheet of paper: "Good Jew," "Faithful Christian," "Obedient Muslim," "Perfect Hindu," and "Enlightened Buddhist."

➤ Invite the group to write on each outline the characteristics of the person named.

Standing My Ground

➤ Ask these questions:

Do you accept the Christian understanding of sin and grace? Why? Why not?

What has Jesus meant for your life?

What has God's love meant for your life?

Worship

➤ Say this prayer:
Lord God of all the universe: we have sinned and fallen short of your glory. You made us all from the dust of the earth; we have feet of clay. None of us is perfect. We break easily. Teach us to dance in your grace with our brothers and sisters in faith. Help us to be the best we can be, in your love. Amen.

➤ Invite the group to sing "He's Got the Whole World in His Hands."

A Book Like No Other

PURPOSE: *To help youth understand the role and value of the sacred writings of Christianity, Judaism, and Islam*

Preparation

➤ The article "Scriptures of the World's Religions" (pages 49-52) will shed light on this program.

➤ Before the meeting, photocopy the Scripture test (see "What's the Big Deal?") so that everyone will have a copy. Tape on the wall three large sheets of paper.

➤ You will need the following materials: a sheet of posterboard; felt-tip markers; a Bible for each participant; Bible commentaries for **Genesis, Isaiah**, and **Luke**. If possible, obtain from a public library a copy of the Qu'ran.

What's the Big Deal?

➤ Invite the youth to take a Bible test to determine how much they know and how much they care (if they care) about the Bible. Distribute pencils and copies of "Bible Survey."

BIBLE SURVEY

Decide if each statement is true (T) or false (F).

1. The Bible is a moldy old book nobody cares about anymore.

2. Paul was one of Jesus' disciples.

3. Moses brought pairs of animals into the ark to save them from the flood.

4. I think the Bible is a little outdated.

5. Ruth moved to a new land with Naomi Judd.

6. Shadrach, Meshach, and Abednego survived a fiery furnace.

7. Jesus was born in Nazareth.

8. Jacob was pretty sneaky, but God had a use for him.

9. Stephen was the first Christian martyr.

10. Stephen was killed by a firing squad.

Answers:
1. F   2. F   3. F   4. (opinion)   5. F
6. T   7. F   8. T   9. T   10. F

➤ Ask the following questions:

What questions do you bring to the Bible?

What answers do you think the Bible should provide?

Does the Bible answer the questions you ask about your life?

➤ Summarize the following information:

Most religions have scriptures that answer questions about the beginning and end of time, tell about the life and teachings of holy people, and define what people in the community of faith should believe and how they should live. Some religions believe that their scriptures are holy in only one language and should not be translated. Missionary religions, which actively try to reach new converts, believe that their scriptures ought to be available in all languages.

➤ Ask the youth:

Which of the world's religions—Hinduism, Judaism, Buddhism, Christianity, Islam—are missionary religions? (only Christianity)

Alive Through the Centuries

➤ Distribute Bibles. Ask the youth to read **Luke 15:11-32**. Discuss the following questions:

Is the father, the younger son, or the older son most like you? Which of their approaches to life is closest to the way you feel about your life?

If you did what the prodigal son did, would your parents be as forgiving as the father? Why? Why not?

What are the issues in the story that are similar to issues you face today? (being jealous, messing up and wanting to make things right, needing to be loved unconditionally, making good decisions, searching for what to do with your life)

Why do people today love the parable of the prodigal son, which was told by Jesus 2000 years ago?

Alive in This Century

Some people think that the Bible is irrelevant because it does not address today's issues, such as drug abuse or violence in the schools. A little digging will show that many of the same underlying issues are in the Bible.

➤ Invite the participants to form small groups. Assign each group a Scripture passage.

➤ Feel free to add to the list of Scripture readings. The issues listed in parentheses are ways of connecting the passages to today's world. Do not mention them until after the participants have tried to identify the issues.

➤ Provide Bibles and commentaries. Ask the members of each group to read and research their assigned passage. Then invite them to list, illustrate, or act out the issues in the story that are similar to issues today.

■ **Genesis 3:1-24** Adam, Eve, the Serpent, and the Apple (Issues: blaming; lying; wanting to know about God, but not knowing how to find out; passing the buck; facing consequences; finding comfort in a bad situation)

■ **Deuteronomy 5:1-21** Receiving the Law at Mt. Sinai (Issues: knowing what God expects, knowing how to fit in, understanding the rules for living, knowing that you are a part of something bigger than yourself)

■ **Ruth** Ruth's Adventures with Naomi and in Bethlehem (Issues: loyalty in the family, coping with losing someone important, figuring out the options for future, handling disappointment, learning new ways, receiving and giving kindness, following instructions from someone more knowledgeable than you are, knowing when and how to do the right thing)

■ **Jeremiah 1:4-10** God's Call to Jeremiah (Issues: knowing that God has a place and a ministry for you, knowing that you are important because of who you are, being scared or uncertain about doing what God wants, making excuses, being brave)

➤ Ask the youth:

How can you use what you have learned from studying the Bible to find help for other issues in your life?

Search for Truth

The Hebrew Bible is made up of three parts, the *Torah* (Law), *Naviim* (Prophets), and *Kethuvim* (Writings). For the most part, the Hebrew Bible corresponds with the Christian Old Testament. In the early part of the Common Era, the Jews added the *Mishnah* and the *Gemara*, which make up the *Talmud* (Learning). There are also commentaries that interpret the Torah. It is not possible to read only the Old Testament and know what it means to be a Jew. Over the centuries, study and interpretation of the scripture have expanded the meaning of Jewish faith and life.

The Christian Bible is composed of two parts: the Old Testament, or Hebrew Bible, and the New Testament. Christians interpret much of the Hebrew Bible in light of Jesus' life, death, and resurrection. Although Christians hold a wide variety of beliefs about the interpretation of Scripture, the Bible is considered the highest authority or the Word of God.

Muslims believe that the sacred writings of Christians and Jews were early revelations from God, which they believe but do not accept as authoritative. They believe that the real Torah, Psalms, and Gospel no longer exist and that the ones we have contain errors and misinterpretations. However, they accept the truth of the Qu'ran in every detail. The Qu'ran was given to the prophet Muhammad by the angel Gabriel, and it supersedes all scriptures that existed before. There can be no critical interpretation of the Qu'ran, and in order to be true, it must be recited in Arabic.

Three Travelers

➤ Summarize "Search for Truth." Say to the class: "Jews, Christians, and Muslims share many of the same stories, but they interpret them differently."

➤ Read **Genesis 22:1-14.** Then read from the Qu'ran **Sura** (chapter) **37:100-109**:

My Lord, grant me a doer of good deeds.
So We gave him the good news of a forebearing son.
But when he became of (age to) work with him, he said: O my son, I have seen in a dream that I should sacrifice thee; so consider what thou seest. He said: O my father do as thou art commanded; if Allah please, thou wilt find me patient.
So when they both submitted and he had thrown him down upon his forehead,
And We called out to him saying, O Abraham,
Thou has indeed fulfilled the vision. Thus do We reward the doers of good.

Surely this is a manifest trial.
And We ransomed him with a great sacrifice.
And We granted him among the later generations (the salutation).
Peace be to Abraham!

➤ After comparing the readings, explain that the Muslims were talking about an attempt to sacrifice Ishmael, Abraham's firstborn son, rather than Isaac.

➤ Read aloud **Luke 1:26-35**. Then read about the birth of Jesus from the Qu'ran, **Sura 3:44-46**:

When the angels said: O Mary, surely Allah gives thee good news with a word from Him (of one) whose name is the Messiah, Jesus, son of Mary, worthy of regard in this world and the Hereafter, and of those who are drawn nigh (to Allah),
And he will speak to the people when in the cradle and when of old age, and (he will be) one of the good ones.
She said: My Lord, how can I have a son and a man has not yet touched me? He said: Even so; Allah creates what He pleases. When He decrees a matter, He only says to it, Be, and it is.

➤ Ask the following questions:

Are you surprised to discover that Muslims recognize Jesus as a great prophet but not as the Son of God? Why? Why not?

The Qu'ran suggests that Mary was a virgin, but Muslims do not say that anything happened outside the laws of nature. They do say that "Allah creates what He pleases," that the virgin birth could have happened. Do Christians believe that Jesus was the Son of God because of the virgin birth? What are other reasons for believing that Jesus was the Son of God?

➤ Read **Isaiah 11:1-5**. Ask at least one or two people to research the passage in a commentary. Then discuss the following questions:

If you were a Jew, how would you interpret Isaiah 11:1-5? Has the person described in the Scripture already come or will he come in the future?

How do Christians interpret the Scripture? Who was Isaiah talking about?

If you were a Muslim, would you find truth in the passage? Who would Isaiah have been talking about?

Hip Hop Scripture

➤ If you have done all the previous exercises, take a break here. Play some active music, such as "Jesus Loves Me, Mon" from the audiotape or CD *Youth! Praise*. If you know a line dance or other motions to use with the music, encourage the youth to get up and moving.

What Is Truth?

➤ Summarize the following information:

When Jesus was standing before Pilate, who held the power to condemn him to death, he said "For this I was born, and for this I came into the world, to testify to the truth." And Pilate asked him, "What is truth?" (**John 18:37b, 38**) At some time in our lives, most of us ask Pilate's question, "What is truth?" All three religions claim to have a corner on the truth, and their scriptures confirm their belief. The Jews call themselves the chosen people, who have a God-given right to claim the land of Canaan. The Christians claim that Jesus is the long-awaited Messiah, who has come to save the world. Muslims believe the Qu'ran is God's last and true statement to the world.

➤ Discuss the following questions, asking the youth to explain their answers:

How do you know when something is true?

How do you know when scripture is true?

Can all scripture contain some element of truth?

Is it OK to argue with another person's scripture?

Is it OK to laugh at his or her scripture?

Why doesn't God make it clear who is right?

Defending the Truth

➤ Divide the class into three groups. Choose one youth to be a devil's advocate who can't believe the stories and who questions the believers. The members of each group will tell an extraordinary story from the tradition they represent. Then the stranger, who has never heard the story, will ask them to defend its truth.

GROUP 1: JEWS
In the Exodus story, Moses encountered God in a burning bush that didn't burn up (**Exodus 3:1-6**). He knocked a stick on a rock and made the rock gush water (**Exodus 17:1-7**). He prayed for bread, and bread fell from the sky (**Exodus 16**).

GROUP 2: CHRISTIANS
Jesus died a grisly death on a cross. His body lay in a tomb for three days, and then he rose from the dead (**Luke 23:26—24:12**).

GROUP 3: MUSLIMS

The perfect man, Adam, was created by Allah from dust, symbolizing the meek character of man. The angels submit to him, except for the jinn (devils) who are created from fire. Man is also fashioned from "sounding clay, of black mud fashioned into shape" (**Qu'ran, Suras 7:11-12** and **15:26-30**).

➤ After each group has defended the truth of its tradition, ask:

> What does thinking that your scriptures are true mean for you and for your daily life?

> How did you feel about defending the story? Was it easier to defend the Jewish and Christian stories than the Muslim one? Why? Why not?

> Why do most scriptures include miracle and creation stories?

Authority Speaks

➤ Say: "The question of the authority of scripture is a thorny one, especially for Christians. Before we can begin to think about the authority of scripture, we should consider the underlying questions."

➤ Write at the top of a sheet of posterboard the title, "Sacred Writings." Then draw vertical lines to make four columns and horizontal lines to make seven rows. Write at the top of the columns "Jews," Christians," and "Muslims." Write in the left-hand column the following questions (but not the answers):

1. Who is considered the source of sacred writing? (Jews: God; Christians: God; Muslims: Allah)

2. Who did God use to write the scripture? (Jews: Moses, prophets, and others; Christians: many people; Muslims: angel Gabriel to Muhammad)

3. Who decided what was authentic and what to keep in the canon? (Jews: rabbis; Christians: third-century church council; Muslims: Muhammad and Uthman, a caliph who organized the effort to collect the oral sayings into a single text by about 650 C.E.)

4. Can the scripture be expanded? (Jews: Yes; Christians: No; Muslims: No)

5. Can you argue with the scripture? (Jews: Yes; Christians: Yes; Muslims: No)

6. Can the scripture be interpreted? (Jews: Yes; Christians: Yes; Muslims: Yes)

7. Who can interpret the scripture? (Jews: rabbis; Christians: anybody; Muslims: believers)

➤ Invite the youth to fill in the chart by answering the questions. Then review the answers.

The Bible and Me

➤ Have a contest to see who can name the most books of the Bible. Then see if anybody can name them in order.

➤ Ask the youth to name the ways the Bible can be used in daily life. Write their answers on a chalkboard or on a large sheet of paper.

➤ Invite the youth to recite their favorite passages. Talk about why they are favorites. Then discuss:

> Is the Bible important for your life? Why? Why not?

> What does the Bible say to youth today? In what ways is the Bible's message unique?

> How can reading the Bible help you in your life?

> What tools can you use to help you read the Bible?

The Bible for Life

➤ Read aloud the following scenarios. Invite the group members to talk about how the Bible and a relationship with the people of the Bible might help the person described in each senario. Encourage the participants to read the suggested Scripture passages.

■ Eli is a confused young man. His parents divorced when he was three; both parents remarried. He grew close to both stepparents. Now his father is divorcing again. (See **Matthew 6:9-15;** the Lord's Prayer, forgiving as we are forgiven by God).

■ Kalil is confused about life. He is not sure if he believes what his parents believe about the Bible. He is not even sure he believes what they believe about God. Does the Bible accept people who doubt? (See **John 20:19-29;** Thomas doubts, and Jesus satisfies his curiosity and adds a blessing to those who believe in faith.)

■ Curtis wants to find a way out. He lives in a rough neighborhood, and the local gang has been putting pressure on him. By selling drugs he could make enough money to get out. (See **1 Corinthians 6:9-11;** wrongdoers will not inherit the kingdom of heaven.)

■ Jeresica is a straight-A student, who is trying desperately to please her parents, her friends, and her church. But she feels empty inside. (See **John 15:1-11;** living in God's grace and pleasing God bring fullness and joy.)

Worship

➤ Read **Psalm 113.**

➤ Conclude the session by playing "Jesus Loves Me, Mon" and inviting the youth to participate in a line dance.

TEACHING ARTICLES

Photo by Skjold Photographs

Scriptures of the World's Religions

Scripture is a writing or, more usually, a collection of writings that a religious community declares to be its holy book. Scripture may tell about the beginning and end of time or about the life and teachings of a variety of holy people, but especially the founder of the tradition. It may also define what people in the religious community believe and how they should live.

Some faith communities believe that their scriptures are divine revelation, that they were directly given by God or that the people who received them were divinely inspired. Other religions believe that their scriptures were written by wise and holy people who had special insight into truth and reality. Whether received through revelation or from holy people, scripture is the supreme authority for worship, doctrine, and behavior. It is read and recited in public worship; and it is studied, read, memorized, and meditated on by individuals looking for devotional and spiritual edification. Scriptures are often revealed in a sacred language and must be maintained in that language. Other scriptures, especially those of missionary religions, can and should be translated and disseminated.

Scripture is usually canonized—that is, its content is determined once and for all by the community. Most scriptures are a closed canon; once the community makes a decision about the content of scripture, nothing can be added to or taken away from it. Many scriptures were transmitted orally long before they were written down.

Scriptures need to be interpreted by the community, so commentaries and theories of interpretation develop and are used by the community to understand and apply the scripture. In recent times and primarily in Western traditions, theories of interpretation, such as historical and literary criticism, have been developed and applied to the study of scriptures. Some people, liberals or modernists, accept the new ways of interpreting scripture; but others, conservatives or fundamentalists, reject them and affirm traditional interpretations.

Judaism

The Hebrew Bible, thirty-nine books, is known by the acronym TANAKH. The consonants in TANAKH stand for the names of the three parts of the scripture: *Torah* (Law, the five books of Moses), *Navi'im* (Prophets, twenty-one prophetic books), and *Kethuvim* (Writings, thirteen books of various literary genre). The books of the Hebrew Bible were written over a period of more than a thousand years and were accepted as a single canon early in the Common Era. TANAKH is also known as the Written Torah, and its Hebrew texts are treated with great respect. Torah scrolls are handwritten by scribes, they are kept covered in the ark in the front of the synagogue, and they are read as the high point of the worship service. The reader uses a special pointer so as not to touch the page.

In addition to the Written Torah, there is the Oral Torah, which Jews believe was revealed to Moses at Mount Sinai and was passed on in oral form until it was gradually recorded first in the *Mishnah* (third century C.E.) and then in the *Gemara* (seventh century C.E.). The Mishnah and the Gemara form the *Talmud* (Learning), which has been the basis for legal, philosophical, and ethical thinking in Judaism. Over the centuries, rabbis, Jewish teachers, have developed and are still developing the Midrash, Codes, Responsa, and Commentaries for the purpose of interpreting and applying the Torah to daily life. Studying the Torah is one of the main activities of any serious Jew.

Modern interpretations of the Hebrew Bible vary. Orthodox Jews are concerned with observing, without omission or compromise, all the teachings and laws of both the Written and the Oral Torah. In contrast, the Reform position is that not all of the laws are binding on contemporary Jews in the same way the ethical teachings are. Reform Jews give more weight to the Written Torah over against the Oral Torah. The Orthodox always read the Torah in Hebrew, whereas the Reform read it in English to facilitate understanding.

Christianity

The Christian Bible is composed of two parts: the Old Testament and the New Testament. The Old Testament is the same text as the Hebrew Bible, although the books are in a slightly different order. Early Christians understood themselves as belonging to the Jewish tradition, which held the books of the Torah, Prophets, and Writings as scripture. Of course, Christians interpreted the same texts differently. They understood the messianic prophecies to be fulfilled in Jesus and only parts of the Law to be binding for Christians.

The New Testament contains twenty-seven books, produced by the early church as a testimony to Jesus Christ. It contains four gospels or accounts of the life and teachings of Jesus; Acts, a history of the early church; and twenty-two letters and tracts, about half of which are

attributed to Paul. Most of the writings of the New Testament are attributed either to the original Apostles, eyewitnesses to Jesus' ministry, and Paul or to their disciples or missionary companions.

Christians talk about the Old and the New Testaments because of their particular understanding of God's covenant-making activities. The Hebrew Bible comprises God's old or original covenant; the new covenant is given in Jesus Christ's life, death, and resurrection, which fulfills and supersedes the old covenant. (It should be clear that the term *Old Testament* is a Christian designation and is not accepted by Jews. Many Christians now refer to the Old Testament as the Hebrew Bible.)

All Christians agree that the Bible is the Word of God and that it is the highest authority in matters of faith and practice, although interpretations of its meaning may vary widely. Orthodox Christians and the Roman Catholic Church have affirmed both that the Church has the authority to interpret Scripture and that the Bible needs to be interpreted by the Church. Protestant reformers stated that the Bible is the sole authority for Christians and that it should be interpreted by each individual. In the modern period, understandings of biblical interpretation are more apt to be divided between a fundamentalist position and acceptance of literary-critical methods for the study of Scripture.

Islam

Islam sees itself as the fulfillment of revelations given earlier to Jews and Christians. Islam believes that God gave scripture to particular prophets: the Torah to Prophet Moses, the Psalms to Prophet David, the Gospel to Prophet Jesus, and finally the Qur'an to Prophet Muhammad. The Qur'an admonishes Muslims to believe in all the Prophets and all the sacred scriptures given to them. However, Muslims claim that the *original* Torah, Psalms, and Gospel of the Prophets no longer exist and that the present ones contain errors and misinterpretations. Therefore, Muslims do not accept the Jewish and Christian scriptures as they now stand. In contrast, they affirm that the Qur'an is true in every detail; that it has experienced no corruption; and that in its Arabic version, it is exactly like the original copy that is with God in heaven.

The *Qur'an* (Recitation) is composed of 114 *Surahs* (chapters), some of which are long and some quite short. Its sacred language is Arabic; and although it has been translated, it is the true Qur'an only in Arabic. When it is recited in prayers and worship, it must be recited in Arabic. Among Muslims, public recitation of the Qur'an is a highly developed and prized skill.

The content of the Qur'an was revealed to Prophet Muhammad through the Angel Gabriel beginning in 610 C.E. and ending with the Prophet's death in 632. Within a decade after Muhammad's death, the present text was established and authorized and the Surahs were arranged in their present order, from the longest to the shortest. The Qur'an contains short versions of many of the stories in the Hebrew Bible; references to Prophet Jesus and Mary, his mother; moral exhortations; and laws. Many commentaries have been written to interpret the Qur'an even though Islam has steadfastly rejected criticism of the text, especially by non-fundamentalists. Qur'anic schools for young children, where the Qur'an is memorized, are found throughout the Islamic world.

Hinduism

In Hinduism, there are two types of sacred writings: *Sruti* and *Smriti*. Sruti is revelation; its texts were heard in ages past by *rishis* or wise men. Smriti is tradition; it contains ideas and teachings of religious value that were conceived by humans and have been passed on from generation to generation.

The best known texts of the Sruti are the *Vedas* and *Upanishads*. There are four Vedas, which contain hymns and poems dedicated to various gods and to the seed of all later religious knowledge and wisdom. The Upanishads are the culmination and completion of the Vedas. They are philosophical treatises that describe the way to enlightenment and liberation through wisdom. There are about a dozen major Upanishads, and they are even now the pinnacle of Hindu thought and the basis of all later philosophical interpretations. The Sruti can be dated from 1200 to 400 B.C.E.

The Smriti is larger and more diverse and is not a closed canon. Although its content is not precisely delineated, most Hindus agree that it contains two great epics, *Mahabharata* (the longest book in the world) and the *Ramayana*. Within the Mahabharata is perhaps the most popular and influential book in Hinduism, the *Bhagavad Gita* (Song of the Lord [Krishna]). It teaches the way of liberation through disciplined activity and devotion to God.

Smriti also contains legal codes, *Puranas* (stories of gods like Krishna and Shiva), sectarian scriptures, and the writings of the six schools of philosophy. The Vedas are written in Sanskrit, a sacred language; the Smriti is written in Sanskrit and in many other Indian languages and dialects. The Vedas are the highest authority in Hinduism, but most people cannot understand their archaic language. The priests and scholars know the language and use it in worship. The epics and Puranas are more popular, although they lack the formal authority of the Vedas.

Buddhism

Each of the three branches of Buddhism—Theravada, Mahayana, and Vajrayana—has its own canon. Each is actually more like a library than a single text. At the Fifth Buddhist Council in Burma, in 1871, the Theravada scriptures were engraved on 729 stones. The Chinese canon contains nearly 100,000 pages of printed text.

THE THREE BASKETS OF THERAVADA SCRIPTURE

The Theravada scripture is known as *Tipitaka* (Three Baskets), and its sacred language is Pali. It has three parts or "baskets": *Vinaya, Sutta,* and *Abhidhamma*. Vinaya contains rules and regulations for the organization of the Buddhist community (Sangha) and for the lives of monks and nuns. The Sutta contains sermons and discourses of the Buddha and is the most important text. Theravadins believe that the Sutta contains the actual words of the Buddha. The Abhidhamma is a later part of the canon and gives philosophical and psychological interpretations of the Buddha's teachings. The Tipitaka is authoritative for Theravada life and practice; worship consists primarily of monks' recitation of the scriptures in Pali.

MAHAYANA SCRIPTURE

The Mahayana accept the Tipitaka as scripture, but they believe that other later writings are equally meaningful and true. The Mahayana canon includes many other *sutras* (later teachings of the Buddha) and *shastras* (commentaries and explanations of the Buddha's teachings), which are written in Sanskrit rather than in Pali. As Mahayana moved into East Asia, many Chinese and Japanese works were added to the canon. Theoretically, the Mahayana canon is not closed, so other writings can be added as truth continues to be discovered.

VAJRAYANA SCRIPTURE

Vajrayana accepts both the Tipitaka and most Mahayana writings as introductory, for people at the early stages of Buddhist truth. Vajrayana accepts a third body of texts, called *Tantra*, which were written in or translated into Tibetan. The Vajrayana canon consists of two parts, the *Kanjur* (sutras) and the *Tanjur* (commentaries). In Vajrayana, they are believed to contain the highest and most esoteric teachings of the Buddha.

For Further Reflection

Use the following questions and activities to reflect on the key points of the article:

SCRIPTURE

What is scripture?

What are some of the ways a community of faith receives its scripture?

A VARIETY OF SCRIPTURES

All religious groups have their own scriptures, which they believe to be correct and sufficient for faith and life.

➤ Make a chart. List down the left side of a sheet of paper each of the religious groups discussed in the article. Write across the top headings that correspond to these questions:

How are the writings organized? (testaments, canons, commentaries)

Was there a holy person who was essential to either giving or receiving the scriptures? Who?

What is the main purpose of the sacred writing? (rules for right living, revelation of God)

➤ Use the chart to summarize and sort out what people in each religion believe about their sacred writings.

THE VARIETY WITHIN THE CANON

Within a religion's scripture, there is often more than one type of canon or testament. The Bible has an Old and New Testament, Hindu writings include Sruti and Smriti, each branch of Buddhism has its own canon, and Judaism has an oral and a written Torah.

➤ Discuss these questions:

Do you think that one part of scripture can contradict another part? Why? Why not?

Why, do you think, are there varieties of expression within some sacred writings?

Do you think that certain parts of scripture are more true than others are? Why? Why not?

How do you assess the truthfulness, meaning, or value of the scripture in your tradition?

For Further Study

See the program "A Book Like No Other" (pages 44-47) for more information and activities about Christian, Jewish, and Islamic scriptures.

JUDAISM

Today Judaism is numerically small; but it is one of the oldest of the world's religions, and it has given birth to two of the largest religions: Christianity and Islam. There are about 13 million Jews worldwide: about 5 million in North America, about 5 million in Israel, and the rest primarily in Eastern Europe and Russia.

What Do Jews Believe?

First and foremost, Jews believe that God is one. The Shema, which they often recite, says, "Hear, O Israel: the LORD is our God, the LORD alone" (**Deuteronomy 6:4**). In fact, monotheism, the belief in one God, is one of the great contributions that Jews have made to human culture. For many Jews, the name of God (spelled YHWH or Yahweh) is too holy to write or pronounce, so they refer to God as Adonai or Lord. They believe that God created the world and that the world is innately good.

Jews believe that God makes covenants—that is, God relates to people by promising to be their God and asking them to do certain things as their part of the relationship. God made a covenant with the whole human race, as well as with all living things, through Noah (**Genesis 6–9**). In the covenant with Abraham and Abraham's descendants, the Jewish people, God promised the blessing of land, progeny, and God's presence (**Genesis 15 and 17**). God renewed the covenant with the Jews by giving the Torah to them through Moses (**Exodus 19 and 20**). Jews believe that they are God's chosen people and that special gifts are given to them, special responsibilities placed upon them, and special suffering required of them.

Jews believe that people are made in God's image and are therefore free and responsible moral agents. Jews do not believe in original sin because they believe that as God's creation, people are innately good. They believe that people are put in the world to take care of God's creation. They are called to live lives of purity and holiness and to work for the repair or redemption of the whole world.

Judaism as a Way of Life

Judaism is more an ethical way of life than a system of beliefs and theology. A Jew is defined more by the way he or she lives than by the beliefs he or she holds. For example, in Judaism there is no clear belief about the nature of an afterlife. Most Jews have a messianic hope, but they differ in the nature of their hope. Some believe that the messiah will be a person; but most believe that in the messianic age, the world will be renewed and all people will live in peace.

Jews believe that although God does not enter history as a person (hence they reject Jesus as God), God does work in and through history. Because throughout most of their history the Jewish people have endured intense suffering, they have often asked why God allows them to suffer. They were in bondage in Egypt and in exile in Babylon; they were separated from their sacred land from 70 to 1948 C.E. They have lived in ghettos; suffered pogroms; and most recently and most bitterly, endured the Holocaust in Nazi Germany. History has strained the faith of many, but the Jews continue to be a people and to serve God and their fellow human beings, while many of their questions remain unanswered.

Jewish Sacred Days, Festivals, and Observances

Jews celebrate in many ways. They consider certain times to be sacred or holy. First and foremost is the Sabbath *(Shabbat)*. The Jews believe that God created the world in six days and rested on the seventh day. God commanded the Jews to observe the seventh day, the Sabbath, as a day of rest. So between sundown on Friday and sundown on Saturday, Jews do not work. (Work may be defined differently by different Jews, but all would agree that work is not to be done on the Sabbath.) They may worship at the temple or synagogue, but they observe the Sabbath primarily in their homes.

During the year, Jews celebrate a number of festivals, many of which began as harvest celebrations, but changed as they were associated with historical events in which God interceded for the benefit of the Jewish people. Passover (Pesach) and the Feast of Unleavened Bread occur in the spring and are a time of remembering and reenacting the Exodus, when God set the Jews free from bondage in Egypt. The Seder meal, which recalls the hurried feast eaten before they left Egypt, is one of the high points of the year.

The Feast of Weeks or Pentecost (fifty days after Passover) originally celebrated the harvest of wheat. Near the time of Jesus, it came to be associated with the covenant and with God's giving the Torah to Moses.

Rosh Hashanah (New Year) occurs in the autumn, and Yom Kippur (Day of Atonement) occurs ten days after Rosh Hashanah. On Yom Kippur Jews ask for forgiveness from God, and they grant forgiveness to all those who have wronged them. This is a season for making things right and starting anew. Immediately after Yom Kippur is the Feast of Tabernacles (which is also called Sukkot or the Feast of Booths). The Feast of Tabernacles originally celebrated the harvest of fruit. The ancient Jews constructed huts or tents to symbolize the vineyards and orchards and to recall the time they spent wandering in the wilderness after their exodus from Egypt.

Hanukkah (Festival of Lights) is celebrated in December and is growing in popularity. It commemorates the courage of the Jewish people who reconsecrated the Temple in Jerusalem after it had been desecrated by the Romans in the second century B.C.E. Hanukkah celebrates religious liberty.

In the life span of individuals, Jews celebrate rites of passage. When a boy is thirteen, he comes of age; he celebrates Bar Mitzvah and becomes a Son of the Law. A girl celebrates Bat Mitzvah. This is a proud moment for the family; a time of celebration for the whole community; and for the young man or woman, a time to assume adult responsibilities. Jews also have rituals for the celebration of birth (circumcision of boys on the eighth day), weddings, and funerals.

The Place of Worship and Teaching

In the first century of the Common Era, Jews were dispersed throughout the Roman Empire. They faced the crisis of the destruction of the Temple in Jerusalem (their center for sacrificial worship) and the loss of the Promised Land. While the Jews were socially, religiously, and legally segregated, synagogues replaced the Temple, and Rabbinical Judaism developed. Rabbinical Judaism emphasizes the sanctification of all life through living by Torah and Talmud.

During the last two hundred years, discriminatory laws have been repealed in Western countries, and Jews have gained equality. Since 1948, Israel has become a haven of refuge and a homeland for millions of Jews from all over the world.

Tradition and Reform

Modernity has presented another crisis for the Jewish people. As Jews begin to participate fully in modern culture, a question arises: Can a person give up traditional, rabbinical, Torah- and Talmud-centered Judaism and still be a Jew?

> *Jews see themselves as having a unique covenant relationship with God, but that does not preclude God's relating to other people.*

At one extreme are the Hasidim and Orthodox who hold firmly to the tradition and who see the Torah and Talmud as God's literal revelation. They try to live literally and exactly by the commandments. They speak Yiddish and Hebrew in worship services.

At the other extreme are the more liberal Reform and Reconstructionist movements. The Reform Jews interpret the scriptures (mainly the Torah) as symbolic and metaphorical rather than literal. They emphasize the moral and ethical dimensions of the scripture's teachings. They use English in their services, and they ordain women as rabbis. Reconstructionism sees Judaism as a cultural force in world history rather than as a religion per se.

The Conservative movement takes a moderate position. Conservative Jews are less traditional than the Orthodox, especially in biblical interpretation; but they stop short of the Reform position. They use Hebrew and English in the service and have recently allowed women to be rabbis.

The Uniqueness of Judaism

What is the relationship of Judaism to other religions? Jews see themselves as having a unique covenant relationship with God, but that does not preclude God's relating to other people. Judaism is an ethnic religion, and it does not try to bring other people into its community. Judaism does not pass judgment on other religions, but adherents of the faith desire the freedom to pursue their own religion.

Judaism is difficult to understand because there is no central authority and no single definition of Judaism that all Jews can agree on. For some, Judaism is a religious stance; for others, it is ethnic or cultural or historical. There are secular Jews and nonobservant Jews; but in some sense, they are all Jews.

For Further Reflection

Use the following questions and activities to reflect on the key points in the article:

JEWISH BELIEF

➤ Three major beliefs are mentioned in the article. Review them, then discuss these questions:

Jews are monotheistic; they worship one God. What does monotheism mean to you?

There is only one God, and God is one. What words would you use to describe God as one?

Why do Jews believe that the created world is good? What does *world* mean in this context?

➤ Divide the group into three teams and assign **Genesis 6–9** to one team, **Genesis 15 and 17** to another, and **Exodus 19–20** to the third. Ask the members of each team to read their assigned passage and to read a commentary for additional information. Then discuss these questions:

How would you describe or define a covenant?

What are conditions of the covenant? What are the Hebrews supposed to do or be? What does God promise?

How are the covenants alike? different?

Why do you think there are several covenants?

Jews think of themselves as a chosen people. What are their special gifts? special responsibilities? What special sufferings have been required of them?

➤ Review the story of the fall of the first man and woman (**Genesis 1—3**). Christians understand the story in terms of original sin. Jews do not believe in original sin.

What does being created in the image of God say about your identity? your actions? your beliefs?

What does it mean to be a free moral agent?

How are the responsibilities of a faithful Jew and a faithful Christian alike? different?

JUDAISM AS A WAY OF LIFE

➤ Divide the class into small groups. Ask the members of each group to draw a picture of what life may be like in the messianic age, then combine the pictures in a kind of mural and have the groups describe their image. Then ask:

The messianic age and heaven are not the same, but both are understood as a time when God makes all things right. How does your image of the messianic age compare with your understanding of heaven?

In what ways is Judaism geared more to living an ethical life than to believing particular doctrine?

➤ There is no part of life that a Jewish person hides from God. Ask older group members to read **Psalm 22** and younger group members to read **Psalm 23.** Ask:

What feelings or emotions are expressed in the psalm?

What are the psalmist's concerns?

What does he say to and about God?

Is your relationship with God like the psalmist's? Could it be? Why? Why not?

SACRED DAYS, FESTIVALS, AND OBSERVANCES

On the Sabbath, Jews do not work. According to selected passages in the Torah, work includes conducting business, preparing food, traveling more than a prescribed distance, building a fire, and so on.

➤ Make a ball by tying a tea towel in a knot, or provide the group with a soft ball that can be used indoors. Tell the group to throw the ball from one person to the next.

➤ Each person who touches the ball must state one activity typical of his or her Sabbath. Then ask the group to talk about which activities honor the Jewish sabbath and which violate it. Ask these questions:

What would your sabbath be like if you observed it according to Jewish custom?

What would have to change?

How would you feel about changing?

➤ Tell the group that Jesus participated in all the Jewish festivals. Briefly review the festivals. Then ask these questions:

What is the significance of each celebration?

Which have parallels in your religious observances?

How does an understanding of the festivals in the Jewish tradition enrich your understanding and practice of worship?

➤ Ask volunteers to tell stories about the ways their families observe rites of passage, especially those that mark the transition from childhood to more adult responsibility.

➤ Then point out that in Judaism, the Bar Mitzvah or Bat Mitzvah marks the transition from childhood to adulthood. With the rite of passage, a Jewish teenager is given the religious and social responsibilities and privileges of an adult. Discuss these questions:

What are adult social responsibilities? religious responsibilities?

How does your religion prepare you to assume adult social responsibilities?

For Further Information

See the video *Judaism: The Religion of a People* (24 minutes) available through Ecufilm; call 1-800-251-4091.

Christianity

In the first century of the Common Era, Christianity emerged from Judaism as a world religion. (We speak of the time beginning with the birth of Jesus as the Common Era because Jews and Christians have it in common. Historians of religion use the designation C.E., instead of A.D., which means in the year of Our Lord, because as a theological statement A.D. excludes Jews.) Christianity takes its name and its central beliefs from the life, teachings, death, and resurrection of Jesus. The story of Jesus and the beginnings of Christianity are found in the New Testament.

The Brief Story of Jesus the Christ

Jesus was born of Mary in a stable in Bethlehem. He grew up in Nazareth and became a carpenter. When he was about thirty, he was attracted by the preaching of John the Baptizer. He was baptized by John in the River Jordan and was tempted in the wilderness for forty days. He then began his itinerant ministry: preaching, teaching, and healing. He had twelve disciples and many other followers. After about three years, he was condemned to death by religious and political authorities. On the third day after his death by crucifixion, God raised him; and after appearing to many people, he ascended into heaven. On the day of Pentecost, the Holy Spirit descended on Christians in Jerusalem and they began to preach and to heal, proclaiming the good news of Jesus Christ. The gift of the Spirit marks the traditional birth of the church. Many Christians believe that Jesus will return to earth at the end of time to usher in God's reign.

The Christian Year

The Christian year commemorates the significant events in Jesus' life. Many Christians observe the Christian year. Others do not because they believe that it was not commanded in the Bible.

The Christian year begins four weeks before Christmas with the season of Advent. Advent, which means coming or arrival, is a time of anticipation and of preparation for the birth of Christ. Christmastide begins on the Feast of the Nativity, the true name for Christmas Day, and continues for eleven more days. It celebrates the birth of the Messiah. Christians do not know the actual date of the birth of Jesus, but Western churches celebrate it on December 25 and Eastern churches on January 6.

January 6 is known by many Christians as Epiphany. *Epiphany* means manifestation, in this case the manifestation of God in Jesus Christ. Christians observe Epiphany by commemorating the visit of the magi and/or the baptism of Jesus by John the Baptist. Both are ways in which people, both Jews (John the Baptist) and Gentiles (the magi), publicly acknowledged the coming of God in the person of Jesus.

Depending on the date of Easter, there are six to nine weeks between Epiphany and Ash Wednesday. Ash Wednesday is the first day of the season of Lent, which is approximately seven weeks before Easter. During Lent, Christians prepare themselves, through penitence, for the joy of Easter. The week before Easter is known as Holy Week. It begins with Palm Sunday, which recalls Jesus' entry into Jerusalem. Maundy Thursday commemorates Jesus' last supper with his disciples. *Maundy* means command; at the last supper, Jesus commanded his followers to observe a common meal in his memory. Good Friday recalls the Crucifixion, and Easter Sunday, the resurrection of Christ.

The fifty days of Eastertide conclude with another day of celebration, Pentecost, which commemorates the descent of the Holy Spirit onto the disciples and the birth of the church. Pentecost is the third of the three major festivals of Christian worship. Christmas is the festival of the Incarnation, God's presence in the world as a human being; Easter is the festival of the Resurrection, the victory of life over death for Jesus and for all Christians; and Pentecost is the festival of the continuing presence of God in the church and world.

A Message of Love and Compassion

Jesus proclaimed a message of love and compassion for a lost and suffering humanity, and he called people to prepare themselves for entry into the coming kingdom or reign of God. The message of Jesus was good news, or gospel, for people forgotten by the political and religious establishment. When asked about the greatest commandment, Jesus said, "You shall love the Lord your God with all your heart, and with all your soul, and with all your strength, and with all your mind; and your neighbor as yourself" (**Luke 10:27**).

The gospel includes justice. The love of God is not a warm fuzzy feeling, but a dynamic power that carries a prophetic mandate to care for "the least of these" as well as the greatest. Indeed, the great who have achieved, gained, succeeded at the expense of the poor or the weak will be the least in the kingdom of God.

Who Is Jesus?

Of greater significance to the development of Christian theology was the way Jesus was understood. He was seen as Messiah; *Christ* is the Greek word for messiah, which means anointed one. Christians understood that Jesus fulfilled Jewish hopes for a messiah, as their hopes were expressed in the Old Testament, especially in the prophetic books. Furthermore, Jesus was seen as the presence of God incarnate, God embodied as a human being, and was given titles such as Lord and Son of God. The church struggled to understand and express who Jesus was and how he was related to God.

In the first centuries of church history, church fathers developed doctrines about the Trinity, or one God in three persons: Father, Son, and Holy Spirit. *Father* refers to God who creates and rules the universe. The *Son* is God who appears in human flesh as Jesus Christ (Incarnation). *Holy Spirit* refers to the spiritual presence of God, who works in the church and the world to guide and comfort people. The early church fathers affirmed Jesus as both fully God and fully human, and they understood his death on the cross as the means of forgiveness and redemption for a fallen humanity (Atonement).

The Fracture of Christianity

Christianity developed in different ways in the eastern and western parts of the Roman Empire. (For a more detailed explanation, see "Orthodox Christianity and Roman Catholics" beginning on page 74). The Roman Catholic Church, in the west, split in the eleventh century from what is now the Eastern Orthodox Church. In the sixteenth century, it was fractured as a result of the Protestant Reformation in Europe. Protestant reformers rebelled against the authority of the Pope and tried to correct abuses and to change church practices of their time. They affirmed the Bible as the sole authority for Christian faith and life, salvation by faith alone by the grace of God, and the priesthood of all believers (the idea that every person has direct access to God and that everyone is a priest to everyone else).

Four main traditions grew out of the Reformation: Lutheran, Reformed and Presbyterian, Anglican, and Anabaptists.

About two hundred years later, the Methodist movement, which was begun by John and Charles Wesley, appeared as a reform movement within the Anglican Church. Methodists affirmed the authority of Scripture and tradition and emphasized the warm heart, Christian experience, and the enlightened mind, Christian learning. The Methodist movement soon spread to the New World. The Methodist, Baptist, and Presbyterian churches became the main churches on the American frontier. America has proven to be a haven for religious people of all persuasions and is home to Eastern Orthodox, Roman Catholic, and Protestant Christians as well as to new American religious groups such as the Disciples of Christ and the Pentecostals.

A Common Heritage and Beliefs

In spite of differences among Christian religious groups, they all have certain beliefs and practices in common. All agree that Jesus Christ is the center of the Christian faith, that God is triune (Father, Son, and Holy Spirit), that the Bible is the authoritative Word of God, and that the church is the people of God in Christ. Human beings stand in need of salvation, and salvation is available through the life, death, and resurrection of Jesus Christ. The church has many sacraments, but two are generally accepted: baptism and the Eucharist or Lord's Supper.

The church is the body of Christ, God's continuing presence in the world; the Holy Spirit works through the church to accomplish God's will. The church is called to be an instrument of God's love, working in the world, as Jesus did, to serve the needy. The church exists in every country in the world, and it sees as its mission nothing less than proclaiming the gospel to every human being. There are more than a billion Christians in the world.

Interchurch and Intrachurch Concerns

In the twentieth century, divisions among Christian churches have begun to heal. The Ecumenical Movement has brought many Protestant and Orthodox churches closer together; some Protestant churches, such as the Presbyterians, have merged with other denominations within their traditions. Some Protestant churches have merged with other denominations outside of their traditions to form new churches, such as the United Church of Canada. Since the Second Vatican Council (1962–65), the Roman Catholic Church has entered into serious conversations with both Eastern Orthodox and Protestant churches. And as the mission of the church continues, some Christians are beginning to talk with people from other world religions.

At the same time, partly as a backlash against many twentieth-century developments in all the churches, many conservative or traditional Christians are seeking to recover a traditional understanding of the gospel and to counter what they consider modern and even heretical, or

Jesus proclaimed a message of love and compassion for a lost and suffering humanity, and he called people to prepare themselves for entry into the coming kingdom or reign of God.

erroneous, ideas. Groups attempting to preserve tradition are called fundamentalists or evangelicals or pentecostals.

Protestant fundamentalists affirm the truth and the inerrancy of the Bible (inerrancy means the inability to make a mistake or error); Roman Catholic fundamentalists emphasize the inerrancy of the Pope when he is speaking about official doctrine or teachings of the church. Evangelicals emphasize a warm, personal relationship with Jesus and the importance of bringing people to faith. Pentecostals, who are sometimes called charismatics, emphasize the presence of the Holy Spirit in believers and in the church as an empowering and emotionally-stirring experience. Fundamentalists, evangelicals, and pentecostals are found within Roman Catholicism and in all branches of Protestantism, as well as in separately organized congregations and denominations.

A Survey of Churches and Traditions in North America

"Christian Religious Expressions," which begins on page 73, is a survey of the major Christian traditions and churches that are found in North America today. North America has been a fertile field for the development, growth, and splintering of religions. Indeed, the United States and Canada are home to the most diverse Christian community in the world. In a resource of this length, it is impossible to list and describe all the Christian churches in North America. For information about groups that are not included or for further information about the religious groups described in this resource, check your public or church library for the *Handbook of Denominations in the United States*, by Frank S. Mead and revised by Samuel S. Hill (Abingdon Press, 1990) and/or the current edition of *Yearbook of American & Canadian Churches*. Most of the church membership figures listed in this resource are from the *Yearbook of American & Canadian Churches, 1994*, edited by Kenneth B. Bedell (published and distributed by Abingdon Press).

For Further Reflection

Use the following questions and activities to reflect on the key points in the article.

THE STORY OF JESUS

➤ Read aloud or photocopy and distribute the part of the article that summarizes Jesus' life, death, and resurrection.

➤ When members of the group are familiar with the story, read aloud "The Brief Story of Jesus the Christ." After each sentence, invite group members to add to the story. For example, after you read the first sentence, others in the group may add what they know about Jesus' birth, about Mary, or about Bethlehem.

➤ Either at the end of the story or as you go along, have the group verify in the gospels (Matthew, Mark, Luke, or John) each addition to the story. After the group tells the expanded version, briefly review the story. Ask what information was new to the group and what parts of the story came from tradition rather than from the Bible. (For example, the Bible says nothing about the number or the names of the wise men).

THE SEASONS OF THE CHRISTIAN YEAR

➤ Post seven large sheets of paper or posterboard; distribute felt-tip markers.

➤ Ask volunteers to write on each sheet of paper one of the church seasons. (The seventh sheet of paper will be used to keep score.) Then ask the others in the group to arrange the sheets of paper so that the seasons are in order according to the church year.

➤ Divide the class into teams of three or four people. Read a question about the seasons of the church year. The team that shouts out the correct answer first will receive two points and will write the answer on the appropriate sheet of paper. Any team that answers incorrectly will have two points deducted from its score.

➤ For each season, ask:

How long is the season?

What, if any, is the name of the first day of the season?

What is the significance of the day or season?

What about Jesus does the season celebrate?

WHO WAS JESUS? WHAT DID HE DO?

➤ Ask group members, at random, for quick responses to the question:

What are names or descriptions for Jesus? (Christ, Son of God, Lamb of God, and so on)

➤ List the group's responses on a large sheet of paper. Then ask:

What did Jesus do? (He healed, preached, taught, confronted the religious leaders.)

➤ List the group's responses. Ask volunteers to find in the gospels examples of the names of Jesus and examples of what he did.

THE BEGINNINGS OF PROTESTANTISM

➤ Review the planks in the Reformers' platform (see "The Fracture of Christianity"). Ask these questions:

What does it mean to believe that the Bible is the sole authority for Christian faith and life?

Is the Bible your sole authority? What other sources of authority help shape your decisions as a Christian?

What does "salvation by faith alone by the grace of God" mean to you? (See **Ephesians 2** and a related commentary.)

What is grace? What is an example of grace in your life?

Who are the professional or designated clergy and leaders in your denomination?

What did the Reformers mean by a "priesthood of all believers"? Would they want the congregation to take over all the pastor's responsibilities? Why? Why not?

How do you picture yourself among the "priesthood of believers"? What is an example of what you would do or be?

➤ The Methodist movement was influenced by the Reformation, but began about two hundred years later. Review the four emphases that are known as the Wesleyan Quadrilateral. Ask the following question:

If the Methodist movement emphasized tradition, reason, and experience as well as Scripture, what is the place of Scripture as a source of authority for Methodist Christians?

➤ Ask the group members to choose an issue on which Christians must make choices—such as potentially violent conflicts or dating behavior. Ask:

How would Scripture, tradition, reason, and experience influence your decisions?

Islam

With almost one billion adherents, Islam is one of the largest religions in the world. Islam is usually identified with the Middle East, the place of its origin; and most of the people in the Middle East are Muslims. But the majority of Muslims live in Africa and Asia. Indonesia has the largest Muslim population, and Afghanistan, Bangladesh, and Pakistan are almost one-hundred-percent Muslim. Muslims also constitute a large minority of the population in Eastern Europe, India, China, the Philippines, Russia, and the former republics of the Soviet Union. Through immigration and conversion, more and more people are becoming Muslims; and Islam is growing rapidly in Europe and North America.

The Beginnings of Islam

Islam is both old and new. It was founded during the Seventh Century C.E.; but its adherents believe that Islam began with the creation of the first human being, Adam, who was also the first Prophet of God. (God is called *Allah* in Arabic). *Islam* means submission, and a Muslim is one who submits. The name of the religion, Islam, refers to an action or an attitude that results in the total submission of a person, in every area of his or her life, to the one true God, Allah.

Islam is a younger cousin of Judaism and Christianity. All three religions believe in one God, in Creation, in many prophets whom God has sent into the world, and in an end to human history. Muslims, like Jews, believe so strongly that Allah is One that they reject the Christian idea of a triune God.

Adam, Noah, Abraham, Moses, and David are some of the prophets revered in all three religions. Jesus is honored by Islam as a great prophet, but not as the Son of God. (Muslims reject the Christian idea of Incarnation.) Islam, while accepting as prophets Adam, Noah, Moses, and many others, firmly believes that Muhammad was Allah's final prophet, the Seal of the Prophets, and that the *Qur'an* is Allah's final book. Muhammad is a prophet; he is not Allah or the son of Allah.

> *Muhammad is the final Prophet of Allah or the Seal of the Prophets. Muslims believe that after Muhammad, there will be no more prophets.*

The Life of Muhammad

Prophet Muhammad, the earthly founder of Islam, lived from 570 to 632 C.E. in Mecca and Medina, in what is now Saudi Arabia. He was orphaned early and raised by his uncle. He married and became the manager of his wife's trading business. He spent a lot of time in meditation and prayer; and at the age of forty, Muhammad felt a call to be Allah's prophet. At that time, Muhammad received the first revelation of the Qur'an. Revelations continued throughout his life, transmitted to the prophet through the angel Gabriel. In Mecca, Muhammad began to preach about the absolute unity of the one true God. He also preached a message of doom and judgment upon the idolaters who continued to worship gods and goddesses.

Muhammad angered the leaders of Mecca; and in 622, he was forced to flee from Mecca to Medina. (622 C.E. is the first year of the Islamic calendar.) In Medina, he established the first Islamic community (*Ummah*); and for the next ten years, he consolidated its power. Just before his death, he took control of Mecca and established the pilgrimage to Mecca that continues today as one of the Five Pillars of Islam.

Prophet Muhammad is remembered. 1) He was the final Prophet of Allah or the Seal of the Prophets. Muslims believe that after Muhammad, there will be no more prophets. 2) He was the channel through which the Qur'an was revealed to the world. All prophets perform miracles; the Qur'an was Muhammad's miracle. Muslims also believe that the Qur'an is Allah's final book. 3) Muhammad was the founder of the first Islamic state in Medina and was its ruler for ten years. It remains the model of an Islamic state. 4) His words and actions are remembered by the community and have become examples for the behavior and lifestyle of Muslims. The writings of and about Muhammad are known as *Hadith* (Traditions of the Prophet), and they are memorized and imitated by devout Muslims.

Muslim Beliefs

What do Muslims believe? Traditionally, Islam has six major beliefs: 1) the absolute unity and oneness of Allah, (2) the acceptance of Allah's Prophets, (3) the affirmation of angels as Allah's messengers, (4) the acceptance of all the books that Allah has revealed, (5) the resurrection and judgment at the last day, and (6) predestination (everything happens according to Allah's divine decree). The main point of a Muslim's identity is not so much what he believes as what he does or how he lives. Law is more important to a Muslim than theology.

So how should a Muslim act and live? There are Five Pillars of Islam that define how a Muslim should live. The *first* is to confess and affirm, "There is no God but Allah, and Muhammad is the Prophet of Allah." This is called the *Shahada*, and to say it with sincerity makes one a Muslim. The *second* pillar is to pray at appointed times, five times a day. Muslims pray facing Mecca. They use particular positions (bending at the waist, kneeling, touching the forehead to the floor) and recite verses from the Qur'an. Muslims may pray alone, with their family at home, or with a larger group in public. At noon on Friday, the whole community (*Ummah*) gathers at the Mosque for community prayers and a sermon. The *third* pillar is almsgiving or paying two-and-one-half percent of one's wealth to help those in need in the community. Fasting is the *fourth* pillar. Muslims fast during the lunar month of Ramadan. This means that for the whole month from sunrise to sunset, nothing is to pass through the throat. Muslims who have the means (health, wealth, and opportunity) are expected to make a pilgrimage to the holy city of Mecca at least once in their lifetime. To do so is the *fifth* pillar of Islam.

The Jihad or Holy War

A so-called sixth pillar is known as Jihad or Holy War. Recently it has been a source of misunderstanding and enmity between the West and the Muslim world. *Jihad* actually means struggle, and its basic meaning refers to a person's struggle with evil tendencies within himself or herself. It also refers to the struggle between an Islamic state and an evil force that is set upon the destruction of Allah's community and Allah's word. When faced with such a situation, a Muslim is required to do everything in his or her power to prevent the victory of evil over Islam. War is required if all other steps fail.

Jihad can be waged only by a true Islamic state and

only after certain conditions have been met. It should be fought in as humane a way as possible. The problem is that many would-be Muslims use the Jihad as an excuse for terrorism and war. Not everyone who shouts *Jihad* has the support of the Islamic community, nor does every act of terrorism or war meet the test of a true Jihad. Most Muslims are peace-loving; but they will not allow anyone to insult, threaten, or destroy their religion.

Islam as a Way of Life

Islam is a way of life rather than a religion. That is, Muslims are to submit to Allah and Allah's word (Qur'an) and Allah's law (Sharia) in every aspect of their family and social lives, their political and economic affairs, and even the details of their personal lives. Every aspect of life should be lived in obedience to Allah's will. Islam does not have priests or ordained clergy, and as a result, has no sacraments as such. But festivals are held at the end of the month of fasting. And during the pilgrimage an animal sacrifice is made to commemorate Abraham's sacrifice of an animal instead of his son.

Islam Today: The Sects *

Islam exists in many different countries and cultures throughout the world. Religious customs and traditions reflect the variety of cultures. However, Islam believes that Allah, the Prophet, and the Qur'an, which bind all Muslims together, are greater than the local cultural differences that divide them. Muslims emphasize the unity of their community.

Just as Christianity is divided into different denominations, Islam is divided by many sects. Muhammad himself warned against divisions among his followers. The location of these sects may help explain some of the recent conflict in the Middle East.

■ About 85% of Muslims are Sunnis (or Sunnites); they follow the Sunna, the six books of traditions. Sunnis believers are orthodox (traditional) Muslims.

■ The Sufism movement follows the mystical and devotional teachings of Islam. Muslim monks are called sufis; they believe that knowledge of God comes directly to the soul that loves him above all else and that waits patiently before him. They are found around the world.

Muslims are to submit to Allah and Allah's word (Qur'an) and Allah's law (Sharia) in every aspect of their family and social lives, their political and economic affairs, and even the details of their personal lives.

■ The *Wahhabi* or *Ikhwan* movement is usually described as being "Puritan"—no ornaments, music, amusements. They have also strongly opposed the Sufi movement. They are mostly found in Saudi Arabia.

■ The *Shi'a* (or more commonly known as Shi'ite) sect is the largest minority. They believe that Muslim leaders must be descendants of Muhammad. The Shi'a brand of Islam is the state religion of Iran. Most people in both Iran and Iraq belong to the Shi'a sect (although Saddam Hussein and his party were Sunni). *Ayatollah* is a title given the greatest scholars in the Shi'a sect.

■ The *Ismailis*, an offshoot of the Shi'a sect, are considered extremists. Members of this sect are scattered throughout Asia and northern Africa.

■ One of the most successful offshoots of Shi'a is now a world religion in its own right—*Baha'i*. The origins of this faith date back to only the middle of the nineteenth century. Baha'i followers are still persecuted in Iran today.

---

* The information in "Islam Today: The Sects," beginning with paragraph 2, has been reprinted from "Islam: The faith of 1/7th of the World," *The Magazine for Christian Youth!*, September 1991, page 39. © Copyright 1991 by Cokesbury.

For Further Reflection

Use the following questions and activities to reflect on the key points in the article:

THE BEGINNINGS OF ISLAM

Islam is one of three monotheistic world religions that began in the Middle East and have common roots. Discuss these questions:

Who are some of the people significant to Islam that are also important to Judaism and Christianity?

In Islam, what is the position of those three people?

As a Christian, how do you think and feel about the fact that Muslims, Jews, and Christians all revere Moses as a great prophet?

As a Christian, how do you think and feel about the fact that all three revere Jesus? Is your response different for Jesus than for Moses? Why? Why not?

THE LIFE OF MUHAMMAD

Muhammad, like Jesus, began his prophetic work late in life. At the age of forty, he received in his first revelation the call to be a prophet.

➤ Say to the group: "Imagine that you were orphaned at the age of six, shuffled among several relatives, and finally raised by a wealthy uncle. Imagine that you are intelligent, but functionally illiterate."

➤ Then ask the members of the group to stay in character and to formulate a mental picture of themselves at age fifty-five or sixty. They should include possibilities for career, marriage and family, social obligations and responsibilities, religious beliefs and activities. (Younger youth may need guidance, so offer them several choices in each category.)

➤ Finally, ask the youth to imagine that an angel has revealed God's call for them to be prophets and that they will have many future revelations. Then ask these questions:

How much did you accomplish in your imaginary life? (Remember, you couldn't read.)

What did you think and feel about the angel's revelation? Did you think it was authentic? Why? Why not?

If you obeyed the revelation, how would it affect your career? your family? your community obligations? How did you feel about its effect on your life?

➤ Review the parallels between Muhammad's life and the participants' imaginary lives. Talk about what Muhammad accomplished.

WHAT DO MUSLIMS BELIEVE?

➤ Review the six major beliefs of Islam. Then ask these questions:

What are the six major beliefs?

What similar beliefs underlie Judaism? Christianity?

What is the connection between a Muslim's beliefs and his or her actions?

➤ Review the Five Pillars of Islam and discuss these questions:

What is the first pillar? How do you think reciting the Shahada makes a person a Muslim?

If you recited, "There is no God but God, and Jesus is God's Son," would you be a Christian? Why? Why not?

What is the prayer life of a Muslim? How is it like your prayer life? How is it different? What does Islam say to you about steadfastness in prayer?

How do Muslims aid people who are in need? How do you help people who are in need?

How would almsgiving affect your community? Would you have to be a Muslim to contribute? Why? Why not?

For a Muslim, what is the purpose of fasting? Are there times of fasting for Christians? What are they?

What is the purpose of a pilgrimage to Mecca? What are other holy pilgrimages that you know about?

What would be a holy place for you to visit? Why would it be important to you?

THE JIHAD OR HOLY WAR

➤ Ask the participants to call out activities, both real and stereotypical, that they believe Muslims do. List on the chalkboard or on a large sheet of paper brief descriptions of the activities. Then ask:

Which activities constitute an act of holy war? Why?

➤ Review the true characteristics of holy war. Then ask:

How accurate were your perceptions of jihad?

How does your understanding of jihad affect your view of Islam and Muslims?

For Further Information

See the video *Islam: The People and the Faith* (22 minutes) available through Ecufilm; call 1-800-251-4091.

Hinduism

Hinduism is the religion of about eighty-five percent of the people of India. Hindu is actually a name given to the religion by people who are not Indians. The people of India usually refer to it as *Sanatana Dharma* or Eternal Truth. As Eternal Truth, the religion is universal. Anyone who seeks the Eternal Truth is Hindu, no matter what his or her religious or national affiliation. However, the two most common criteria for identifying a Hindu are these: He or she accepts the authority of the sacred scriptures known as the *Vedas*, and he or she belongs to one of the castes of India.

To Be a Hindu

Hinduism is a religion, actually a way of life, that has no historic founder and has flourished in India for thousands of years. Hinduism and Indian culture are so inextricably intertwined that it is almost impossible to differentiate between them. Hinduism is not a missionary religion, and it is difficult for a person who is not an Indian to become a Hindu. Hinduism has undergone many changes in its history, but it is still a strong and growing religion among the people of India.

Hinduism has no central church or authority or creed. Hindus have many different beliefs, and they worship different gods and read different scriptures; but they all affirm that the highest calling of all Hindus is to fulfill their social role to the best of their ability, to strive for liberation in the way appropriate to their disposition and needs, and to grow ever closer to the Eternal Truth.

> *The two most common criteria for identifying a Hindu are these: He or she accepts the authority of the sacred scriptures known as the Vedas, and he or she belongs to one of the castes of India.*

The Concept of God

Most Hindus believe in god, but the word means different things to different people. For some philosophical mystics, god is the highest reality and the deepest truth. God is impersonal and beyond name and form. The philosophers call god Brahman. For others, god has a name, form, and personality.

Some of the most popular gods are *Brahma* (creator), *Shiva* (destroyer), *Vishnu* (sustainer), and the mother goddess *Shakti*, all of whom appear in many forms. Shiva is a powerful, but loving, god. Vishnu appears in the world in many forms for the purpose of preserving good and destroying evil. The best known human forms of Vishnu are Rama and Krishna. Rama is the ideal human being; *Krishna* is portrayed as an infant, a boy, a handsome youth, a husband, and a prince. Hindus worship god in female form as the goddess, for they believe that god is greater than human ideas of gender. Some forms of god are animals.

The worship of god is called *puja*. In worship, a priest chants scriptures; the devoted offer gifts of food and flowers, and they dress and decorate an image of the god. Though they express devotion to a variety of gods, Hindus realize that all the names and forms of god they worship are really expressions of the one true reality (Brahman), which is beyond name and form.

Ultimate Reality, Karma, and Salvation

Hindus do not believe in one creation and destruction of the world; they believe in endless cycles of creation and destruction. Each cycle begins with creation by the god Brahma. The universe is maintained by the god Vishnu, although conditions gradually decline until finally, when it is beyond repair, the god Shiva destroys it. Then another creation occurs and the process starts all over again. The cycles have no absolute beginning and will have no final end.

Hindus believe that Ultimate Reality is one, eternal, and changeless. In the universe, the Ultimate Reality is called *Brahman* (world soul). The same reality in every living being is called *Atman* (individual soul). Hindus affirm that Brahman and Atman are not different. That is, the essence of each living being is the same as the essence of the universe.

Hindus believe that the Atman lives in a body and that a person's Atman is reborn again and again according to his or her past karma. The cycle of rebirth is known as the transmigration of souls (not as reincarnation, since incarnation generally refers to the various forms taken by gods and goddesses).

Hindus believe that in the cycle of rebirth their present condition is caused by their previous actions and that their future state will be determined by the actions they take in the present. The total effect of a person's actions is known as karma and determines his or her destiny. The ultimate goal of Hinduism is to attain *moksha* (freedom), when a person's karma is perfect (all good works and no evil) and he or she leaves the wheel of life. In salvation, the Atman is set free from all limitations to be one with Brahman again. Moksha can be pursued in various ways or *margas*. Often the ways are meshed. People are to choose the way or ways that best suit their temperament and needs.

THE WAY OF ACTIVITY: KARMA MARGA

Activity, or doing good works, is practiced daily by millions of Hindus. The way of activity centers chiefly on offering gifts and sacrifices to the gods, goddesses, or spirits, through worship (*puja*) in the temple or at home shrines.

In the temple is the stored power of the gods. The priest, or Brahmin, is in charge of temple ceremonies that feed, bathe, decorate, and commune with the deity. Brahman can set free the power of the deity. Wealthy Hindus may build their own ornate temples as signs of devotion, thus aggregating greater good works or merit.

THE WAY OF KNOWLEDGE: JNANA MARGA

The way of knowledge is a more difficult path than the way of activity, for it requires a single-minded devotion and great sacrifice to attain the final step of becoming a holy man.

A Hindu man's life has traditionally been divided into four stages: student; householder; forest dweller; and, for a few individuals, holy man. Virtually all Hindus will take the first two steps, but the man who pursues the way of knowledge is required to take the third and fourth steps as well. The stages on the way to knowledge are somewhat blurred today, although there is still a sense in which each stage of life defines a person's attitude. The duty of a student is to study and learn the sacred literature, while the duty of a married householder is to be a responsible husband, father, and citizen. The third stage,

*Hindus believe that
in the cycle of rebirth
their present condition
is caused by
their previous actions
and that their future state
will be determined
by the actions they take
in the present.
The total effect
of a person's actions
is known as karma
and determines
his or her destiny.*

forest dweller, is not a duty, like the first two stages, but a choice. If a man continues on the way of knowledge, he leaves his home, business, and family in the good care of his sons and becomes a forest dweller. He becomes the disciple of a guru and learns the meditative and ascetic life. The fourth stage is becoming a holy man, using the meditative techniques (yoga) learned from the guru. One of the techniques of the ascetic life is self-mortification, such as lying on a bed of thorns. Self-mortification helps the Hindu man achieve the necessary concentration for yoga. Through his intense concentration, he hones the virtues needed to attain the final level of holiness that will lead to salvation or moksha. Since the way of knowledge is so intense, not many choose to follow it.

THE WAY OF DEVOTION: BHAKTI MARGA

The third way is through devotion and is the most popular pursuit of moksha. One need not build a shrine or enlist the aid of a priest to offer devotion. The Hindu chooses one of the gods or goddesses as his personal deity and the object of his love and devotion. In return, the gods offer grace to provide good karma, which then breaks the cycles of transmigration of the soul. Vishnu, Shiva, Shakti, and Krishna (or one of their incarnations) are the gods most often chosen.

The Caste System

For centuries in Hindu society, caste has been the basis of social relationships. Contact between members of different castes, or social classes, is strictly controlled. At the present time, discrimination on the basis of caste is illegal in India; and in the urban areas and among more progressive Indians, caste is of little importance. However, in the rural villages of India and among the more traditional people, the caste system defines the way people relate to one another, especially in intimate relationships, when people eat together or marry.

Caste also plays a significant part in the Hindu pursuit of moksha. Hindus believe that in the transmigration of the soul, a person's karma determines his or her caste. There are five castes or classes in Hindu society. The most privileged is the *Brahmin* or priest. The second is *Kshatriya*, the warrior or governing class, followed by *Vaisya*, the middle class of merchants and tradesman. The fourth caste is *Sudra*, the peasantry, farmers and manual laborers. The lowest caste is outcasts or untouchables, who perform the lowliest occupations and have no access to the rituals of the other classes.

Being in one caste or another is not unjust; a person's karma determines his or her social standing. And while there is no intermingling, a faithful Hindu, through the pursuit of moksha and the attainment of good karma, may reach a higher caste in the next transmigration of his or her soul.

For Further Reflection

Use the following questions and activities to reflect on the key points in the article:

THE HINDU CONCEPT OF GOD

Hindus believe in one Ultimate Reality (Brahman or world soul) and in many gods (one of which is Brahma) who take various forms, human and animal, male and female. The priest, a Brahmin, offers worship to the gods, such as Brahma, to attain unity with Brahman. (See, there's a good reason why you were confused!)

➤ Review "The Concept of God" and clarify who's who: Brahman is the Ultimate Reality; Brahma is a god; Brahmin is a priest.

➤ If possible, obtain from your local library one or two books that include pictures of some of the Hindu gods and goddesses. Show them to the participants. If you don't have pictures, invite someone to present to the class verbal pictures of the gods and goddesses. Then ask these questions:

What do the Hindu gods look like? What characteristics do their appearances suggest?

Why are there several gods instead of one, as in Christianity or Judaism, or none, as in Buddhism?

Although God is neither male nor female, Christians often think of God as male. How would having female gods affect your concept of deity?

In what ways, if any, do Christians offer food, flowers, or other material things to God? What is the difference between the Christian offering and the offering to a Hindu god?

ULTIMATE REALITY, KARMA, SALVATION

➤ Ask the participants to draw a picture or chart that will help them review the process of salvation that leads to moksha. Be sure they define their terms and understand how karma, moksha, and Ultimate Reality interrelate. Then ask these questions:

What is karma? Do people who are not Hindus have karma? Why? Why not?

How does the cycle of rebirth work?

How does a person attain moksha?

Is it possible to have a perfect karma? Why? Why not?

Can Christians attain perfect goodness? Why? Why not? What does perfection mean to you?

Do people who are not Hindus have Atman? Is Atman called by another name? If so, is it linked in some way to Brahman? How is the Hindu understanding of Atman like the Christian's idea of a soul? In what ways is Brahman like God?

THE WAYS TO SALVATION OR MOKSHA

➤ Review the ways of activity, knowledge, and devotion. Spend some extra time sorting out the way of knowledge.

➤ Invite the participants to imagine that they are Hindus. Ask them to choose a way and to plan how they would pursue it. What would they do? (Remember: Women can't be holy men!)

➤ Then discuss these questions:

What way did you choose? Why?

How are the ways to moksha and a Christian life of discipleship similar? How are they different?

If love, salvation, and unity with Ultimate Reality are the goals of life, does it make a difference if you are a Hindu or a Christian? Why? Why not?

THE CASTE SYSTEM

➤ Review the five castes. Assign each person a caste. Assign castes so that the group is representative of the community they live in. For example, if most people in the community are professionals, assign most of the participants to Kshatriya, the warrior or governing class, and to Vaisya, the middle class of tradesmen. If the community is largely a farming area, most of the participants should be in the fourth caste, Sudra.

➤ Ask each person to review the way to moksha that he or she chose. Remind him or her to consider the effect of a person's caste on his or her opportunities and ask him or her to change plans as necessary.

➤ Invite the members of the group to discuss their plans with one another, but be sure they do not break any rules of the caste system (no intermingling). Then ask these questions:

How would you feel about having your religious life tied to your economic or social position?

Why is caste so influential in the Hindu way of life?

In the United States, is caste or social class related to the ways we practice our religion? Why? Why not?

What does Jesus teach about a person's faith, discipleship, and position in life? How is Christianity like Hinduism? How is it different?

For Further Information

See the video *Hinduism: An Ancient Path in the Modern World* (about 21 minutes) available through Ecufilm; call 1-800-251-4091.

Buddhism

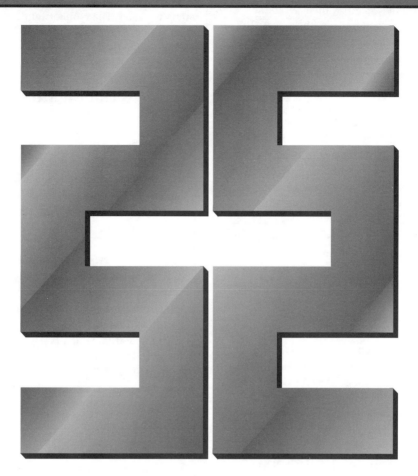

Buddhism is a world religion that is found primarily in Southeast and East Asia. In the Twentieth Century, Buddhism has suffered from the advance of Communism, especially in China, Tibet, North Korea, Vietnam, Laos, and Cambodia. At the same time, Buddhism is growing in North America because of refugees from Tibet and through the work of missionaries from other Buddhist countries. Many Theravada, Zen, and Tibetan monasteries, temples, and meditation centers have been established in North America, bringing the number of Buddhists in the world to over three hundred million.

The Three Divisions of Buddhism

Buddhism is divided into three main groups: Theravada, Mahayana, and Vajrayana.

Theravada means the way of the elders or monks, and it offers salvation to monks alone. People in this group see themselves preserving the true teachings of the Buddha and transmitting them faithfully from the time of the Buddha until today, 2,500 years later. Theravada is located primarily in Burma (Myanmar), Cambodia (Kampuchea), Laos, Sri Lanka (Ceylon), and Thailand.

Though Theravada is the older form of Buddhism, it is known as the Little Vehicle.

Mahayana, the Great Vehicle, developed around the beginning of the Christian era. It incorporated new beliefs and practices, added more writings to the scriptures, and expanded the community to include laity as well as monks. Mahayana elevated the figure of Buddha to a transcendent and divine being and affirmed the presence of many Buddhas beyond the earthly Buddha, Gautama. Mahayana developed as the human ideal the *Bodhisattva*, a being whose life is characterized by wisdom and compassion and who remains in the world, forgoing Nirvana, to save a suffering humanity. Mahayana is found primarily in China, Japan, Korea, and Vietnam. Zen is a popular school of Mahayana Buddhism.

Vajrayana is the most recently developed form of Buddhism, and it emphasizes elaborate rituals and rigorous meditation. It is found mainly in Tibet, although its leader, the Dalai Lama, now lives in exile in India.

Although the three forms of Buddhism are quite different, they all believe in the Buddha, the Buddha's teachings, and the community of monks and nuns.

The Beginnings of Buddhism

Who was the Buddha? His name was Siddhartha Gautama, and he lived from about 563 to 483 B.C.E. in the northern part of India. He grew up as an Indian prince in privileged and sheltered circumstances. But as a young man, he ventured out and saw the negative aspects of life, such as sickness, old age, and death. He also learned about people who renounced the world in order to search for an answer to the problem of human suffering.

Gautama was well acquainted with the precepts of Hinduism and eventually reformed it into a new movement under his leadership. At the age of twenty-nine, Gautama decided to follow the Hindu course of renunciation. Leaving his wife and young son, he spent six years wandering, begging, fasting, studying, thinking, and meditating. Finally, after great struggles and temptations and after rejecting as unsatisfactory some of his Hindu beliefs, he became enlightened; he woke up. (*Buddha* means enlightenment or one who has awakened.) After his enlightenment, he gathered followers and taught them until his death at eighty years of age.

Buddhists believe that because of his enlightenment, he was not reborn but entered into a state of peace called Nirvana. Buddha was a pathfinder, an example, a teacher, and an inspiration; but he was not a god or a savior. The most holy pilgrimage sites for Buddhists are the places in northern India where the Buddha was born, where he was enlightened, where he preached his first sermon, and where he died.

The Teachings of Buddhism

The Buddha's teachings are contained in the scripture called *Tipitaka* (Three Baskets). Buddhism is known as the Middle Way, the avoidance of extreme asceticism and self-denial on the one hand and of luxury and self-indulgence on the other.

Central to the teachings are the Four Noble Truths, which describe Buddhism's view of the world. The *first* is that life in this world is precarious, undependable, changing, decaying, temporary; it has no eternal essence. In short, life is full of suffering. Buddhists believe in seeing life realistically.

The *second* is that people suffer because they desire something that life can't give. They become attached to the things of the world, which are unreliable; so people are always disappointed. The human problem is that we always want what we can't have; and if we could have what we want, it would not satisfy us.

The first two truths are the bad news, but the *third* is good news. Giving up desire and attachment to the things of the world can end suffering and bring about joy. Nirvana is the state of bliss brought about by the end of suffering. (Nirvana is not a place like heaven. It is the absence of desire, attachment, suffering, greed, anger, and delusion.)

The *fourth* Noble Truth explains that by walking the Noble Eightfold Path a person can resolve suffering and attain Nirvana. The Noble Eightfold Path is divided into right beliefs or resolves, the moral life, and the mystical or meditative life.

The Eightfold Path

RIGHT BELIEFS

1. Right Understanding, which is knowing the truth, seeing the world as it really is.
2. Right Thought, which is purity of mind with no thought of hate, lust, jealousy, or illusion; but with positive thoughts of love and truth, which break the wheel of becoming.

RIGHT MORALITY

3. Right Speech, which is purity of words and speech, avoiding lies, gossip, and meaningless chatter. (If you do not have something good to say, don't say anything.)
4. Right Action, which is purity of behavior and involves following the five moral and ethical precepts: Do not kill (respect all life). Do not lie (speak only the truth). Do not steal or take what does not belong to you. Do not misuse sex. Do not use intoxicants.
5. Right Livelihood, which is purity of vocation and involves making sure that your job or career does not cause you to harm anyone.

RIGHT MEDITATION

6. Right Effort, which is setting goals and striving for them with energy.
7. Right Meditation
8. Right Concentration, which means, by right meditation, purifying the mind, controlling and disciplining the mind, focusing the mind, and becoming fully attentive to everything that you do.

By following the Eightfold Path, a person can increase in wisdom, morality, and meditation and thus move closer to the experience of Nirvana. Otherwise, he or she will continue in the endless cycle of death and rebirth. Perhaps the simplest statement of the Eightfold Path is this: Avoid evil; do good; purify your mind.

As people mature in their progress on the path toward Nirvana, Buddhism calls them to four kinds of love: 1) loving kindness for all creatures (human, animal, and otherwise) and wishing well-being for all creatures in all things; 2) compassion for those who are less

> *Buddhism is not so much a formal religion as a way of life, which is open to anyone who experiences suffering and wishes to find peace of mind. An adherent of Buddhism does not join an organization; he or she chooses to walk the noble path and to conform to the discipline of the noble truths.*

fortunate than they are; (3) joy and respect for those who are more fortunate than they are; and (4) equanimity in the face of upsetting and troubling situations.

Buddhism as a Way of Life

Buddhism is not so much a formal religion as a way of life, which is open to anyone who experiences suffering and wishes to find peace of mind. An adherent of Buddhism does not join an organization; he or she chooses to walk the noble path and to conform to the discipline of the noble truths. Buddhism does not believe in an almighty creator god to whom one prays for benefits. The problems people experience are their own problems; they caused them, and they alone can solve them. Buddhism believes that things happen as a result of a person's past actions (karma), not because of God's punishment and not because of fate. In addition, a person's future is determined, at least in part, by his or her present actions, not by the grace or the wrath of God. Buddhism is a radical way of self-help in which a person depends entirely on his or her own efforts to stop personal suffering.

Buddhism in the Community

There is also in Buddhism the community of monks and nuns (primarily monks today), who have given up their lives of worldly involvement (marriage, family, career, position, and wealth) and have taken upon themselves the monastic life. They have vowed to live a disciplined life dedicated to their own spiritual growth as well as to teaching and serving the laity. Because of their separation from worldly activities, they are dependent on the laity for food, shelter, clothing, and medical care. In spite of, or perhaps because of, the dedication and sacrifice of becoming a monk, one of the most meaningful events in the life of a boy and his family is his entering the monastery. He may become a monk for a short period of time or for his lifetime. The event is like an initiation into manhood, and it brings great merit on the family.

Most Buddhist festivals celebrate events in the life of the Buddha. For example, in Southeast Asia, the celebration of the birth, enlightenment, and death of the Buddha is on the day of the full moon in May.

For Further Reflection

Use the following questions and activities to reflect on the key points in the article:

THE BEGINNINGS OF BUDDHISM

➤ Review the significant events in Siddhartha Gautama's life. Note the circumstances of his childhood, young adulthood, quest for enlightenment, and subsequent life. Then ask the following questions:

What was Gautama's early life like? What made him decide to change?

How would you describe his enlightenment?

If you led a life of privilege could you give it up to seek enlightenment? How is seeking enlightenment like being called by God to a life of discipleship?

What are the similarities and differences between Gautama's path to enlightenment and Jesus Christ's life and ministry?

THE TEACHINGS OF BUDDHA

➤ Explain that Buddhism teaches a middle way between the extremes of asceticism and self-indulgence. Discuss these questions:

What is asceticism? Why would it interfere with a life of devotion?

What is extreme self-indulgence? Why would it interfere with a life of devotion?

➤ Divide the class into three groups. Assign one of the Four Noble Truths to each group. Do not ask the participants to deal with the Eightfold Path at this time.

➤ Ask the members of each group to draw, sing, dramatize, rap, or use another creative method of expressing the Noble Truth they have been assigned.

➤ Invite the groups to show and tell about what they have done.

➤ If you have enough time, suggest that **older youth** read and research **Ecclesiastes 6** and **James 4:1-12**. Then ask:

How are the ideas expressed in these passages like the first three Noble Truths? How are they different?

What other passages in the Bible speak to the ideas expressed in the Noble Truths?

Can a sacred truth in one religion be a sacred truth in another? Why? Why not? What are examples of truths that are accepted by more than one religion?

THE FOURTH NOBLE TRUTH: FOLLOWING THE EIGHTFOLD PATH

➤ Assign to each small group, one of the three divisions of the eightfold path: Right Beliefs, Right Morality, Right Meditation. Ask each group to consider these questions:

How would you describe each path to Nirvana?

What are the goals and effects of following each path?

In what ways is the Buddha's teaching about the Eightfold Path like Christian teachings? How is it different?

Is the Eightfold Path compatible with Christian beliefs? Why? Why not?

NIRVANA AND SALVATION

One difference between Christianity and Buddhism is the idea of Nirvana, which is not a place like heaven, but an end to suffering. Another difference is that Buddhists think of salvation as the result of a person's own effort; Christians think of salvation as an act of God.

➤ Review the information in the section "Buddhism as a Way of Life." (For a more in-depth discussion of karma see the article on "Hinduism," which begins on page 65.)

➤ Ask participants to consider the meaning of Nirvana and the ways to attain Nirvana. Then invite them to create, paraphrase, or borrow song titles or bumper stickers to summarize what they've learned. (These may be humorous, but should not be disrespectful.)

➤ Bring the participants together to tell about their titles or bumper stickers. Then discuss these questions:

Is Buddha a god? If not, what role does he have in life? in an afterlife?

How does a Buddhist attain salvation? How does the Buddhist understanding of salvation differ from the Christian understanding?

In heaven, people will be one with God and will no longer experience suffering; how is heaven different from Nirvana?

For a Buddhist, what role do good works play in the attainment of salvation? What role do they play for a Christian? If salvation is not the result of good works, why should we bother to do good works?

Do you think that the end of suffering is the same as salvation? Why? Why not?

For Further Information

See the video *Buddhism: The Middle Way* (about 25 minutes) available through Ecufilm; call 1-800-251-4091.

Christian
Religious
Expressions

Roman Catholic and Eastern Orthodox Churches

The Christian church began in New Testament times with the evangelizing work of the disciples and apostles of Jesus Christ. As the good news spread, converts formed fellowship groups in their homes; then they formed congregations and eventually church groups with leaders called *presbyters*, or elders, and deacons. By the end of the second century, the pastoral offices became part of a structured ministry, in which ministers were ordained, or set apart, and bishops, overseers, presided over the churches in particular areas.

In 325 C.E., bishops from all over the Christian world met at Nicaea, a small town in what is now Turkey, and hammered out a statement of beliefs about the nature of God and the church. Their statement became the Nicene Creed.

The Christian church grew for nearly one thousand years before significant cultural and political differences led to a major breach. The church was so large that it crossed many nations and included many different peoples, languages, and cultures. The church in the West, centered in Rome, used Latin in worship and in the conduct of business. The church in the East was centered in, but not ruled from, Constantinople (now Istanbul, Turkey); it employed the Greek language. The cultural differences, in addition to political and theological differences, brought the tension between the two ancient Christian traditions to a breaking point.

The church in the West insisted on strict organizational unity and was led by the pope in Rome. The word *pope* comes from the Latin word meaning papa or father; sometimes the pope is called the Holy Father. Obedience to Rome and to the pope was a condition of legitimacy; the true church was the Roman Church. In deference to the supremacy of the pope in Rome, the western church became known as the Roman Catholic (universal) Church.

On the other hand, bishops in the East believed that true unity was found not in rigid compliance with Roman authority, but in the continuity of belief. Teaching and being faithful to the historic doctrines of the church would be the foundation of Christian unity. *Orthodoxy* means correct belief. Christianity in the East became known as the Eastern Orthodox Church.

The Great Schism, the first formal breach between the western and eastern churches, occurred in 1050 B.C. Worldwide Christian unity came to an end. In the West, now Europe, the pope's control and authority increased

> *The church in the West insisted on strict organizational unity and was led by the pope in Rome. Bishops in the East believed that teaching and being faithful to the historic doctrines of the church would be the foundation of Christian unity.*

in matters of organization and faith. The Eastern Orthodox, while insisting on a common framework of belief, allowed independent government of the churches within nations or among ethnic groups. Eastern Orthodox Churches were in the area that is today Greece, Turkey, Russia, Serbia, Rumania, Bulgaria, Georgia, and Albania. So within Eastern Orthodoxy there emerged the Greek Orthodox Church, the Russian Orthodox Church, and so forth. Christians who emigrated to North America brought with them the government of their ethnic traditions and the doctrine of Eastern Orthodoxy.

Roman Catholicism: Built upon Peter the Rock

Jesus said to Peter, "You are Peter, and on this rock I will build my church" (**Matthew 16:18**). The name *Peter* means rock. Roman Catholics believe that Jesus intended the Christian church to be built on Peter's leadership. Tradition holds that Peter journeyed to Rome and became bishop of the Christian church there. The Roman Church teaches that when Peter died, his successors, the bishops in Rome who followed him, possessed the same authority and responsibility for leadership of the universal, or catholic, church.

Roman Catholics think of themselves as members of

the original, undivided church. They have a sense of belonging to one another across national boundaries and of having a distinct history. While recognizing other Christians, the Roman Church believes that it is the core of the whole people of God and that the church is united under the authority of the pope.

Eastern Orthodoxy also understands itself to be the continuing presence of the original, undivided church. While it recognizes the pope as the successor to Peter, the bishop of Rome, it rejects the claim that the pope exercises authority over all Christians throughout the world. Protestants do not recognize the pope's jurisdiction either and generally hold that the rock Jesus talked about refers to Peter's faith rather than to his office as bishop of Rome.

The government of the Roman Catholic Church is a hierarchy, a chain of command headed by the pope. Moreover, since 1870, it has been an official teaching of the Roman Catholic Church that when the pope speaks *ex cathedra*, he is infallible in matters of faith and morals. *Ex cathedra* means from the chair or from the authority of his office. *Infallible* means incapable of error. Neither Eastern Orthodox nor Protestants accept the view that the pope is infallible.

The national or ethnic churches of Eastern Orthodoxy are governed by bishops. The bishops of Constantinople, Antioch, Alexandria, Moscow, and Jerusalem have authority over other bishops and are known as patriarchs or fathers. The Ecumenical Patriarch, the patriarch of Constantinople, is the honorary head of the Eastern Church; but he does not function as the pope does.

Sacred Scripture: Written Tradition

Roman Catholics, Eastern Orthodox, and Protestants all teach that the Bible contains the word of God. Roman Catholics and Eastern Orthodox believe that not all the truths delivered by God to the church are contained in the Bible. Some of the teachings of Christ have been passed on to us through the traditions of the church, through the interpretation of the bishops and other church leaders. The recorded traditions of the church are considered to be revealed by God and are regarded as sacred Scripture.

In addition to the sixty-six books of the Bible that are accepted as canon or authoritative by most Protestant churches, the Roman Catholic and Eastern Orthodox Churches also accept the *Deuterocanon* (second canon), which is also called the *Apocrypha* (hidden books). Many of the books of the Apocrypha are thought to be additions to books in the Old Testament and seem to echo its themes and literature. Many Protestants have used the Apocrypha for study, devotion, and preaching. Anglicans and Lutherans continue this practice. None of the books of the Dueterocanon appear in the Jewish Bible.

> *Roman Catholics and Eastern Orthodox single out one saint for special veneration: the Virgin Mary, the mother of Jesus. Because they believe that Jesus Christ is God, they refer to Mary as the Mother of God.*

Mary: Mother of God

Like most Christians, Roman Catholics and Eastern Orthodox honor the saints, the holy ones and heroes of faith. But they single out one saint for special veneration: the Virgin Mary, the mother of Jesus. Because they believe that Jesus Christ is God, they refer to Mary as the Mother of God. Since the church is the body of Christ, Mary is seen as the mother of the church. She is also called the Queen of Peace and the Queen of Heaven. Venerating Mary is not the same as worshiping God, but it does represent a kind of devotion that is unfamiliar to Protestants.

Roman Catholics believe in and teach the doctrine of the Immaculate Conception, that Mary was conceived and born without the stain of original sin. Neither Eastern Orthodox nor Protestants subscribe to the doctrine of the Immaculate Conception. Roman Catholics and Eastern Orthodox believe in the Perpetual Virginity of Mary, that Mary refrained from having sexual relations even after Jesus was born.

Roman Catholics and Eastern Orthodox also believe in the Assumption: When Mary died, she was not buried; instead her physical body was taken up into heaven. Eastern Orthodox believe but do not accept as official dogma Perpetual Virginity or the Assumption. Protestants accept the virgin birth, the idea that Mary was the virgin mother of Jesus; but they reject the notions of Immaculate Conception, Perpetual Virginity, and Assumption.

Roman Catholics and Eastern Orthodox, with many Protestant denominations, believe in the communion of saints, the idea that the Christian community spans every time and place and includes those in Christ who have died, as well as those who are living. Because the saints who have died are still members of the church, Roman Catholics and Eastern Orthodox believe that requesting the prayers of a saint is as natural as asking any other church member for prayers.

The Seven Sacraments

Sacraments are outward and visible signs of inward and spiritual works of grace or God's favor. In the Eastern Orthodox Church, the sacraments are often called mysteries. Most Protestant churches celebrate two sacraments because Scripture records only two that Jesus instituted himself and commanded his disciples to observe: Baptism and the Lord's Supper or Communion,

which is also called the *Eucharist* (thanksgiving). Some churches, like the Baptist churches, use the term *ordinances,* which means commands, rather than *sacraments.* Most Christians believe that baptism washes away the stain of original sin and seals the individual in the body of Christ, the church. It is the one sacrament that practically all Christians practice.

Christians understand the Lord's Supper in a variety of ways. Many Protestant churches teach that the giving and receiving of bread and wine (the juice or fruit of the vine), the elements of Communion, accompanied by Christ's words, is a sign or symbol of the self-giving of Christ as the suffering and living Lord. By sharing a meal in the Lord's name, we remember the death, resurrection, and ascension of Jesus. Roman Catholics usually call the Lord's Supper the Mass, and Eastern Orthodox usually refer to it as the Divine Liturgy. Both believe that when Jesus said, "This is my body; this is my blood," he actually gave himself to the disciples. The Last Supper was true communion with Jesus. The elements of the Eucharist are not symbolic, but the actual body and blood of Jesus.

Penance, which includes confession and absolution, or forgiveness of sins, is often called the reconciliation of the penitent, the person who is sorry for what he or she has done. While Protestants do not generally consider penance a sacrament, reconciliation is practiced in various ways in Protestant churches—for example, through pastoral counseling and through corporate prayers of confession and words of pardon. In the Roman Catholic and Eastern Orthodox Churches, penance is the sacrament through which God heals and forgives people for sins committed after baptism.

Roman Catholics and Eastern Orthodox also celebrate as sacraments *anointing the sick, confirmation,* and *marriage.* Although Protestant churches do not regard them as sacraments, many think of them as sacred or sacramental moments.

Roman Catholics and Eastern Orthodox make more of *ordination* (which means to set apart) than most other Christian churches. They believe that when a person is ordained, he is marked with a character that allows him to act as a representative of Christ. In Roman Catholic and Eastern Orthodox Churches, only males are ordained. Women may participate in other ministries. They may be nuns or lay leaders, but they may not be deacons, priests, or bishops. The Protestant understanding of ordination differs among the churches, but is generally understood as setting apart and empowering a person for ministry to the people of God. Most, but not all, Protestant churches ordain women.

Orthodox Christianity: Heaven on Earth

Because Roman Catholicism and Eastern Orthodoxy were one church for a thousand years, they have a number of elements in common: the Deuterocanon, the veneration of the Virgin Mary, the sacraments, and a male priesthood. But they also have a number of important differences, most of which are differences in degree or emphasis.

First, in the Eastern Orthodox Church the language about God is mysterious, that is, it conveys the majesty and transcendence of God in terms that more often describe what God is not. For example, the Eucharistic prayer speaks of God as inconceivable, invisible, and incomprehensible, yet God is known and present.

While most Christian churches are trinitarian (they believe that God is one and three: Father, Son, and Holy Spirit), the Orthodox emphasize the role and work of the Spirit. God acts throughout all time to bring people to salvation. The aim of the Orthodox Christian's life is to acquire the Holy Spirit.

Second, Orthodox Christians stress the Incarnation, God's coming to humankind in the person of Jesus. They believe that God became human so that humans could become divine. The Eastern Church believes in *deification*, the idea that people have personal access to God and that through prayer and participation in the Eucharist, they can become unified with Christ, who is himself a union of humanity and divinity.

Third, Eastern Orthodoxy is best understood through its elaborate and ancient tradition of worship. Orthodox worship involves all the senses. Music, chanting, colorful icons (two dimensional representations of saints and windows into heaven), and clouds of incense involve all five senses in the Divine Liturgy. The Orthodox achieve in worship a feeling of the presence of God. To participate in the Divine Liturgy is to experience the beauty and majesty of God's heavenly court. The church is heaven on earth. It is the otherworldliness of worship that makes evident God's presence.

Roman Catholic Church in North America

The Roman Catholic Church is the largest religious body in North America, numbering approximately 60 million baptized members in nearly 20,000 parishes, or local churches, in the United States and about 12 million baptized members in over 11,000 parishes in Canada. About one-half of Canadian Roman Catholics are found in the French-speaking province of Quebec. Although priests came with Columbus to the New World, the Roman Catholic Church was established in Canada in 1534 with the arrival of explorers from France and in the United States in 1634 with the founding of St. Mary's in Maryland.

Eastern Orthodoxy in North America

In North America, there are an estimated six million baptized Eastern Orthodox Christians in these main jurisdictions: the Greek Orthodox Archdiocese of North and South America; the Orthodox Church of America, which was formerly known as the Russian Orthodox Church in America; and the jurisdictions representing the Antiochian, Serbian, Rumanian, Bulgarian, and Carpatho-Russian Orthodox churches. Recently, the primary Eastern Orthodox jurisdictions decided to move toward union.

Adapted from "Eastern Orthodoxy: One in the Spirit," by Donald D. Wachenschwanz; *The Magazine for Christian Youth!*, July, 1992; beginning on page 32; and from "Roman Catholics: Christians with Distinctions, by Donald D. Wachenschwanz; *The Magazine for Christian Youth!*, September, 1992, beginning on page 26.

While most Christian churches are trinitarian, the Orthodox emphasize the role and work of the Spirit. God acts throughout all time to bring people to salvation. The aim of the Orthodox Christian's life is to acquire the Holy Spirit.

For Further Reflection

Use the following questions and activities to reflect on the key points of the article:

WORSHIP

➤ If possible, make arrangements for the members of the group to worship with a Roman Catholic and an Eastern Orthodox congregation and then to worship together at your church. Before each visit, encourage the participants to be aware of what they see, hear, smell, touch, and taste. After each visit, invite the group to reflect on their experience. Ask:

> What new or unusual experiences did you have that involved one of your senses? (smelling incense, hearing chanting) What was the experience like?

> How did the involvement of your senses affect your worship experience? In what ways was the worship service like those you usually attend? How was it different?

> Were there aspects of worship at the Roman Catholic or Orthodox service that you would like to add to the worship service at our church? Why? Why not? What aspects of the services at our church help you to worship? Why?

> What does it mean that the aim of Orthodox worship is mystical union with God? What is the aim of our worship service?

SCRIPTURES

The Eastern Orthodox and Roman Catholic Churches include the Apocrypha as part of their Holy Scriptures. Some Bibles include the Apocrypha. Obtain several copies from your pastor or from your local or church library.

➤ Distribute the Bibles. Tell the *younger youth* to look up **Sirach 6:5-17**. Then ask:

> What does the Scripture say about friendship?

> If our church does not consider the Apocrypha to be Scripture, does the passage in Sirach contain God's truth? Why? Why not?

➤ Divide the *older youth* into teams of two. Assign each team one of the following: **1 Esdras 4:13-32, Judith 8, Judges 13.** Ask:

> What did the woman do? What was her role in the story?

> How did the men regard her?

> Who seemed to understand what was going on? How do you know?

> In what ways is the story you read similar to other Bible stories about women? How is it different?

> If our church does not consider the Apocrypha Scripture, do stories in the Apocrypha contain God's truth? Are they worth considering? Why? Why not?

MARY AND THE SAINTS

Roman Catholic and Eastern Orthodox Christians revere Mary as the mother of God. They honor other faithful people as saints. They pray not only in the name of Christ, but also in the name of the saints. Most other Christians pray to God in the name of Jesus Christ; and they respect, but do not revere or pray to, other faithful people. However, reverence for Mary or the saints is not worship in the same sense that God is worshiped.

➤ Have available Bibles and a few concordances. Divide the class into small groups. Ask the members of each group to talk about Mary and other prominent people in the Bible.

➤ Give the youth ten minutes to develop a story about one of the people they talked about. The story should include how the person lived out the teachings of Jesus and/or how he or she experienced the presence of God. (Encourage the teens to read about the person in the Bible.)

➤ Ask a representative from each group to tell about the person his or her group chose. Then ask:

> What is the most significant way in which the person demonstrated his or her faith?

> Was he or she a hero? a saint? Why? Why not? Does his or her being a hero or a saint make a difference in what he or she can teach us about being faithful? Why? Why not?

> What does our church teach about the saints? Who are the saints? Should they be revered? What do you think about the church's teachings?

An Introduction to Protestant Denominations

In the first half of the 1500s, there was widespread concern over the condition of the Roman Catholic Church in Europe. Although the church had undertaken its own reform, some of its leaders had become notoriously corrupt and Rome was exercising heavy-handed political power. People in the nations that emerged from the Middle Ages had a strong sense of national identity. Widespread nationalism fueled demands for reform and independence from Roman domination. Large numbers of people supported reform of the church, but they represented a minority of the Catholics in sixteenth-century Europe. Some of the leaders concerned about reform adopted the name Protestant, which means protesting, in order to distinguish themselves from the Roman Catholic majority.

The Roots of Christian Denominations
The Protestant Reformation

Martin Luther, a Roman Catholic priest and monk in Germany, protested the misuses of church authority. In 1517, he publicly disputed Rome's authority. Other challenges to the church's authority dated back to the fourteenth century, but Luther's public protest is often considered the beginning of the Protestant Reformation. Luther and other reformers—Ulrich Zwingli of Zurich, Switzerland, and John Calvin of Geneva, Switzerland— stressed acceptance of beliefs that became the basis of Protestantism. *First*, sacred Scripture, rather than the pope or sacred tradition, was the highest authority for Christian faith and life. The reformers stressed the need for common people to read the Scripture and to be able to approach God directly without a priest's intervention. The printing press had just been invented, and Luther and other reformers translated the Bible from the Latin into the languages of the common people: German, English, and French. *Second*, the reformers believed in justification, or salvation, by faith in God's promises. Individuals cannot earn salvation by doing good works or acts of piety, such as going to Mass every Sunday. *Third*, the reformers stated that all baptized Christians constituted a priesthood of all believers who had direct and immediate access to God. Clergy were needed as leaders, pastors, and counselors; but priests were not needed as mediators between the people and God.

The reformers set out only to correct abuses within the Roman Catholic Church; it was not their intention to start new churches. However, the pope chose to excommunicate Luther and other Protestant reformers (he denied them the sacraments). Large areas of northern Europe came under Protestant control or influence. The churches of the Reformation, which were Lutheran, Calvinist, and Zwinglian, evolved into or influenced the formation of a variety of churches, which later came to North America. In the United States and Canada, there are over 250 different Protestant denominations.

Adapted from "Families of Faith: Denominational Differences," by Ed Trimmer, *The Magazine for Christian Youth!*, October 1991. © Copyright 1991 by Cokesbury.

Lutheran Churches

On October 31, 1517, a German monk named Martin Luther wrote ninety-five essays describing points of disagreement that he had with the teachings and practice of the Roman Catholic Church. He nailed the essays on the door of the Castle Church in Wittenberg. Luther intended that the essays be used for discussion and debate. But he was eventually branded a heretic and was excommunicated by the Roman Catholic Church.

Martin Luther sought refuge in Wartburg in the castle of a German prince, Elector Frederick. There Luther translated the Bible into German. His translation and commentary further challenged the Roman Catholic Church, its interpretation of Scripture and its ecclesiastical control.

In Germany and in the Scandinavian countries, which are today Denmark, Finland, Iceland, Norway, and Sweden, the Reformation continued in ways suggested by the beliefs of Martin Luther. The reformers focused on preaching the gospel and administering the sacraments in the native language of the people rather than in Latin. Central to Luther's thinking was the idea that people are saved, or made right, by the grace of God alone, not by gifts to the church, manipulation of the clergy, or good works. This concept is called justification or salvation by faith.

Scripture, for Luther, was the ultimate authority in matters of faith and practice; by affirming Scripture alone (*sola scriptura*), he challenged the authority of the clergy. He also challenged their power by asserting that Christians are bound together in a priesthood of all believers and that all Christians are responsible for discipleship and service. Luther and his associates wrote several documents that helped explain their beliefs: the longer and shorter catechisms (1529), the Augsburg Confession (1530), Smalcald Articles of Faith (1537), and the Formula of Concord (1577).

The word *Lutheran* does not refer as much to Martin Luther as it does to an era or a school of thought within Christianity. In Europe, churches in the Lutheran tradition are called Evangelical (which in Europe means Protestant); national Lutheran churches are called the Church of Denmark, the Church of Sweden, and so forth.

North American History

As early as 1619, a Lutheran Christmas service was held in Canada at Hudson Bay. The first congregation of Lutherans in the United States was founded in the late 1630s. Lutherans continued to come to North America in increasing numbers. From 1850 to 1910, almost three million Germans, Swedes, Norwegians, Danes, and Finns

> *Central to Luther's thinking was the idea that people are saved, or made right, by the grace of God alone, not by gifts to the church, manipulation of the clergy, or good works. This concept is called justification or salvation by faith.*

migrated to North America and brought with them their own brands of Lutheranism.

Henry Muhlenberg, who came to America in 1742, is considered the principal organizer of American Lutheranism. Muhlenberg tried to hold in tension the Lutheran concern for correct thinking (correct doctrine and confessional writings) with correct feeling (conversion and application of the faith to the Christian life.) He helped organize Lutheran communities across America.

The first two hundred years of Lutheranism in America was a bewildering picture of denominational disunity, as each church tried to keep its European language, beliefs, and customs. By the early 1900s, Lutherans in America had begun to put their ethnic and theological differences behind them and to unite for specific church ministries, such as mission work.

Evangelical Lutheran Church in America

On January 1, 1988, the Lutheran Church in America, the American Lutheran Church, and the Association of Evangelical Lutheran Churches united into one church. With slightly over five million members, they formed the largest Lutheran body in the United States or Canada.

The Evangelical Lutheran Church in America (ELCA) is the only mainline Protestant denomination that uses the word *evangelical* in its title. At the heart of what Lutherans believe is the *evangel,* the gospel or the good news of the death and resurrection of Jesus Christ for the sins of the world. Evangelical Lutherans place primary importance on creeds and confessions, which explain what Scripture has taught. Lutherans also emphasize that faith comes as God's gift, not as a personal decision. The church accepts biblical criticism (scholarship), ordains women, enters into relationships with other Christian churches, and allows Christians who are not Lutheran to participate in Holy Communion.

There are eleven thousand Lutheran congregations in sixty-five synods in the United States and the Caribbean. The synods are organized into nine regions. A church-wide assembly elects bishops, who function as chief pastors and executive officers for the regions.

Evangelical Lutheran Church in Canada

The Evangelical Lutheran Church in Canada is the Canadian cousin of the Evangelical Lutheran Church in America, and the two churches cooperate closely. The Canadian Church became a denomination in 1985 through the union of the Evangelical Lutheran Church of Canada and the Lutheran Church in America, Canada Section. In the Evangelical Lutheran Church in Canada, there are over two hundred thousand baptized members in over six hundred parishes.

Lutheran Church-Missouri Synod

The second largest Lutheran body in North America, is the Lutheran Church-Missouri Synod. It has just under three million baptized members in over five thousand parishes. Throughout its history, the denomination has been concerned with pure doctrine. It has maintained a strict allegiance to conservative and confessional Lutheranism, which it reaffirmed following doctrinal disputes in the 1970s. The church traces its roots to settlers in Missouri who were concerned not only with doctrinal purity, but also with educating their children in correct ways of believing.

The denomination celebrates closed Communion, which means that only members of the denomination are allowed to partake of the Lord's Supper. It does not ordain women as pastors and usually does not enter into ecumenical relationships with other churches.

Lutheran Church-Canada

The Lutheran Church-Canada is the Canadian counterpart of the Lutheran Church-Missouri Synod. It has approximately 80,000 baptized members in over 300 parishes.

Adapted from "Families of Faith: Lutherans," by Ed Trimmer; *The Magazine for Christian Youth!*, April 1992. © Copyright 1992 by Cokesbury.

For Further Reflection

Use the following questions and activities to reflect on the key points in the article.

THE ROOTS OF THE PROTESTANT REFORMATION

➤ Consider these questions:

Who was Martin Luther? What was going on in the church that he and others didn't like? Why did they object?

What role did Scripture play in the Reformation?

Luther and other reformers translated the Bible into the languages of the people. What changed when people began to worship and to read the Bible in their own languages?

Is the Bible important today as an agent of change? Why? Why not?

What did the pope do in response to the reformers questions and challenges? What does excommunication mean in theory? in practice?

MAJOR LUTHERAN DENOMINATIONS

➤ Ask these questions:

In what ways are the Evangelical Lutheran Church in America and in Canada like the Lutheran Church-Missouri Synod and its Canadian counterpart? How are they different?

What are the issues that define the major Lutheran denominations? Are the same issues important in your denomination?

What is your denominations's stance on biblical inerrancy? ordination of women? ecumenical dialogue? open Communion?

What do you think about these issues?

LUTHERAN BELIEFS AND YOU

➤ Select an issue in Lutheran theology or practice. Have Bibles available for reference. Invite the class to form debate teams. Ask each team to choose a position to defend. Be sure both sides are equally represented.

➤ After the debate, ask these questions:

Did the debate help you to better understand the Lutheran point of view? Did it help to clarify your denomination's position? your own position?

What arguments were the most persuasive? Why were they persuasive?

What Scripture was most helpful in understanding each team's position? Did your team try to understand the theological viewpoint without referring to Scripture? Why?

Presbyterian, Reformed, and United Churches

The family of churches called Presbyterian, Reformed, and United have a common heritage in the Calvinist tradition. John Calvin was a Frenchman who helped to lead the Protestant Reformation from Geneva, Switzerland. As a young man, Calvin was influenced by the teachings of Martin Luther. He broke with Roman Catholicism and systematically worked out what he believed. In 1536, at the age of twenty-seven, he published the first edition of *The Institutes of the Christian Religion.*

The reformed tradition, which includes the Presbyterian Church and some United churches, is based on Calvin's theology. Calvin accepted many of Luther's teachings. He believed in the authority of Scripture and in salvation by the grace of God alone. Calvin's unique contribution to the Reformation came in his emphasis on the sovereignty (the supreme, independent power) of God and also on the redemption of the social order. Calvin was especially concerned that the social, political, economic world be aligned with God's purposes; he spent years in Geneva trying to reform the city so that it would be run as a theocracy, a government ruled by God.

Doctrine

Calvin's whole thought revolved around the concept of God's sovereignty and justice. God, according to Calvin, was the sovereign and eternal ruler of the world. Other people have summarized his theological system in five main points, sometimes called the TULIP doctrine. Over the centuries, Presbyterians have debated and refined Calvin's theology, particularly the meaning of predestination and limited atonement.

■ *Total Depravity.* Calvin believed in original sin. Human beings are completely incapable of being the creatures God expects them to be; people can't help sinning. And even if individuals could keep from sinning, the world, both the natural and the human social order, is totally corrupted by sin.

■ *Unconditional Predestination.* Salvation is unconditional. It is not based on merit, but only on the grace of God through Jesus Christ. Because God is sovereign, God makes the decisions about who is saved and who isn't. Predestination means that God saves us up front, before we can even try to save ourselves. It also means that in all things, God works for good, moving the world toward its final destiny.

■ *Limited Atonement.* Christ's death and resurrection is for the saved, the people chosen by God to be united or reconciled with God.

■ *Irresistible Grace.* Because God is sovereign, people cannot reject or resist God's grace. We are saved because God saves us, period.

■ *Perseverance of the Saints.* Though saved by grace, the church exists in the human, sinful world. Perseverance of the saints simply means hanging in there, trying to live as the people of God in a sinful world.

Sacraments

Presbyterian, Reformed, and United churches believe in two sacraments: Baptism and Communion. A sacrament is a sign and seal of God's grace given in the death and resurrection of Jesus Christ. The sacrament points us to the Christ event, which saves us; the sacrament means that the grace of God is sure. Baptism is a sign that we have already been united with Christ, that we are heirs to the promises of God, and that we are part of God's community. In Communion, we are united with Christ in his death and resurrection. The elements of bread and wine or juice symbolize the body and blood sacrificed by Jesus Christ on our behalf. Christ is thought to be present in the word and sacrament and in the community of faith.

Education

In worship and belief, Presbyterian, Reformed, and United churches try to balance ardor and order. They tend to affirm right thinking and to be suspicious of great outpourings of emotion.

Presbyterians, especially, have been interested in education and have founded a number of colleges and universities. Presbyterian pastors are well educated. In the late 1700s and early 1800s, a large number of Presbyterians came to America from France, England, Scotland, and the Netherlands. They were well represented in both legislative and executive branches of government.

Presbyterian Church Government

The word *presbyterian* comes from a Greek word that means elder. Each church elects lay people to be ruling elders. They serve on the session, which makes most of the decisions about the life and ministry of the congregation. Elders also represent the congregation in the presbytery, a governing body that is composed of ministers and elders representing all the churches in an area. Synods serve larger areas and are usually composed of representatives from four or more presbyteries. The general assembly is the governing body for the national church. The presbyteries, synods, and general assembly serve both a legislative and a judicial function.

Members of a congregation vote to call a minister, or teaching elder, to their church. Ministers are ordained by the presbytery and are members of the presbytery.

Reformed Church Government

Reformed congregations generally employ a modified presbyterian plan of government. The local church is governed by a consistory that is made up of elders, deacons, and pastors. Local churches in a geographical area are grouped into classes (singular: classis). Classes are arranged into regional synods, and the supreme governing body is the general synod.

United Churches:
"That They May Be One" (John 17:11)

In the first part of the twentieth century, groups in several countries, including Australia, Canada, the United Kingdom, and the United States, moved toward uniting Protestant denominations. The movement was especially popular in Canada where, in 1925, the Methodist Church, Canada; the Congregational Union of Canada; the Council of Local Union Churches; and many of the congregations of the Presbyterian Church in Canada merged to form The United Church of Canada. (Presbyterians who have not joined The United Church continue as the Presbyterian Church in Canada.) In 1930, the Wesleyan Methodist Church of Bermuda and in 1968 the Canada Conference of the Evangelical United Brethren became part of the denomination.

In the United States, in 1957, the Congregational Christian Churches and the Evangelical and Reformed Church merged to form the United Church of Christ. A number of local Congregational Christian churches did not enter into the union and chose instead to continue the Congregational Christian tradition; some congregations cooperate with one another through the National Association of Congregational Christian Churches.

While United churches have brought together several Protestant denominations, most have had a direct link with the Calvinist or Reformed tradition. The United Reformed Church in England and Wales is in the United Kingdom. The Church of Scotland and the Presbyterian Church of Ireland are also Reformed in theology and Presbyterian in government, but they are not part of the United Reformed Church.

Government for United churches varies from denomination to denomination and tends to reflect the Congregational and Presbyterian forms of government. In the United Church of Christ, local government varies from church to church and often includes trustees or deacons. Several local congregations are organized into associations, which assist congregations and ordain or certify ministers. Churches in larger geographical areas are organized into conferences; and the general synod attends to constitutional, national, and international concerns. The organization of The United Church of Canada is similar; local congregations are formed into presbyteries, conferences, and a general council.

Presbyterian Church (USA)

In 1861, with the outbreak of the Civil War, the Presbyterian Church in the United States of America split over issues of slavery and states' rights. Most of the southern Presbyterian churches withdrew and constituted their own denomination, which eventually came to be known as the Presbyterian Church in the United States. Through the uniting of a variety of denominations, the northern Presbyterian community became the United Presbyterian Church in the United Sates of America. In 1983, the southern and northern Presbyterian churches reunited to form the Presbyterian Church (USA). With over three million baptized members in over 11,000 congregations, it is the largest Presbyterian denomination in the United States.

Calvin's whole thought revolved around the concept of God's sovereignty and justice. God, according to Calvin, was the sovereign and eternal ruler of the world. Over the centuries, Presbyterians have debated and refined Calvin's theology, particularly the meaning of predestination and limited atonement.

Other American Presbyterian Denominations

The next largest Presbyterian denomination in the United States is the Presbyterian Church in America, with 240,000 baptized members in over 1200 congregations. In 1973, several congregations that were concerned about doctrinal orthodoxy broke away from the Presbyterian Church in the United States, the southern church, to form the Presbyterian Church in America. In 1982, the Reformed Presbyterian Church, Evangelical Synod, merged with the Presbyterian Church in America.

Noted for its commitment to evangelism and mission work, the Presbyterian Church in America takes a strong position on the authority of Scripture and holds strictly to traditional standards of Presbyterianism, particularly to the Westminster Confession of Faith. (Other denominations accept several creeds of the church.) The denomination does not ordain women as deacons, elders, or pastors; and some congregations deny leadership positions to people who have been divorced.

The Cumberland Presbyterian Church, with about 90,000 members in nearly 800 congregations, was organized in Tennessee in the early 1800s. The Cumberland Presbyterians objected to the doctrine of double predestination (some are saved, some aren't) and also wanted to be able to call clergy who were not as highly educated and who would be willing to serve on the frontier.

Presbyterianism is the largest Christian tradition in the Republic of Korea. When Korean Presbyterians immigrate to the United States, many affiliate with one of the older American Presbyterian churches. However, many Korean families have chosen to affiliate with the Korean Presbyterian Church in America.

Other Presbyterian denominations in America include the Associate Reformed Presbyterian Church, Evangelical Presbyterian Church, Orthodox Presbyterian Church, Reformed Presbyterian Church of North America, and Second Cumberland Presbyterian Church in the United States.

Presbyterian Church in Canada

Representing 233,000 baptized members in nearly 1,000 congregations, the Presbyterian Church in Canada consists of the Presbyterian churches that did not unite with the United Church of Canada in 1925.

Reformed Church in America

The Reformed Church in America, which was also known as the Dutch Reformed Church because its earliest members emigrated from The Netherlands, was established in New Amsterdam, New York City, in 1628. It is the oldest continuing Protestant denomination in America. The denomination is solidly rooted in the reformed tradition of the Heidelberg Catechism and other classic reformed statements of faith. It also has a long record of cooperation with other Christian churches. It has 275,000 members in close to 1,000 congregations.

Reformed Church in Canada

The Reformed Church in Canada is the Canadian counterpart of the Reformed Church in America. It has 6,000 members in 42 congregations.

United Church of Christ

The United Church of Christ was formed in 1957 with the union of the Congregational Christian Churches, which were the direct heirs of the Massachusetts Bay Colony Puritans (the pilgrims), and the Evangelical and Reformed Church, which was an American denomination with a German and Swiss-German heritage. The United Church of Christ has more than 1.5 million members in 6,300 congregations. Many local congregations have retained the names they had before the merger, so they may be called, for example, First Congregational Church or Second Evangelical and Reformed Church.

United Church of Canada

The United Church of Canada, which in Canada is usually referred to simply as United Church, is the largest Protestant denomination in Canada and was formed when most of the major Protestant traditions in Canada merged. The major Protestant traditions that did not unite were Anglicans, Baptists, Lutherans, and Pentecostals. Initially, Anglicans had been expected to enter the union as well. The United Church has nearly two million members in over 4,000 congregations. In the national census and in popular surveys, more than two million Canadians identify themselves with the United Church.

Adapted from "Families of Faith: Presbyterians," by Ed Trimmer; *The Magazine for Christian Youth!*, October 1991. Copyright © 1991 by Cokesbury.

For Further Reflection

Use the following questions and activities to reflect on the key points in the article.

➤ Divide the class into five small groups. Assign each group one of the five main points of Presbyterian and Reformed Doctrine. Ask the members of each group to read about, to discuss, and to briefly explain the point of doctrine they have been assigned. Give the groups copies of the following questions to guide their discussion:

GROUP 1:
TOTAL DEPRAVITY

What is sin?

If we say that people inevitably sin, what else are we saying? Can anyone be good? Why? Why not?

What are examples of sin in the natural world? the social order?

Who is accountable for sin in the social order?

GROUP 2:
UNCONDITIONAL PREDESTINATION

Is it possible to earn God's grace by doing good works or by being a good person?

Read **Romans 8:28-29** and **Ephesians 1:3-14**. Do you think that God has chosen some people to save and others to condemn? Why? Why not?

How is the Presbyterian doctrine of predestination similar to what you believe? How is it different?

If God moves the world toward its destiny, does God determine everything we do? Do we have any freedom of choice?

GROUP 3:
LIMITED ATONEMENT

What is atonement?

Is the death and resurrection of Christ for everyone? for some?

What do the Crucifixion and Resurrection have to do with the sins of the world? the natural world? the human social order?

Presbyterians believe that God makes decisions ahead of time about who will be saved. If it were up to you to decide who should be saved, how would you make the decision?

GROUP 4:
IRRESISTIBLE GRACE

What is grace? What passages in the Bible describe or define God's grace?

What does it mean to say that we cannot resist God's grace?

When have you seen the grace of God in your life?

Do you think God's grace can be earned? Why? Why not? How do you feel about grace, which is God's free, unconditional love?

GROUP 5:
PERSEVERANCE OF THE SAINTS

If God has saved us in Jesus Christ, how come the world is such a mess?

How do faithful people live in an unfaithful world?

How do we deal with our own sinfulness?

➤ Bring the groups together to explain the five points of doctrine. Ask:

What does it mean that God is sovereign?

What does the idea of God's sovereignty have to do with the point of doctrine you discussed?

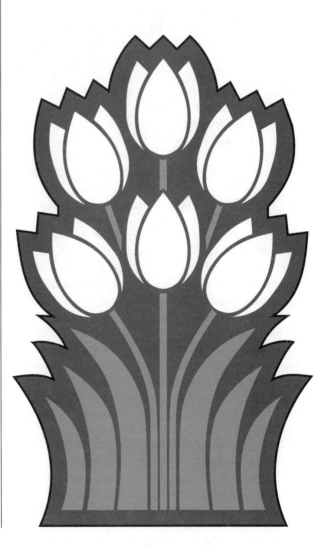

Anglican and Episcopal Churches

The Church of England remained intact after the Reformation, and grew as the British Empire expanded overseas and as missionary activity stretched into lands and cultures whose people did not speak English. (In fact, most Anglicans in the world today do not speak English as their first language.) Two prominent denominations in North America, the Episcopal Church and the Anglican Church of Canada, claim a common heritage in the Church of England.

The Anglican Tradition

The Anglican Church was originally the Church of England (Anglican means English). Until 1543, the English church was part of the Roman Catholic Church. At that time, it recognized the English king, Henry VIII, instead of the pope, as the head of the church in England; and the English church became the Church of England.

The Anglican Church uses the term Protestant to distinguish itself from Roman Catholicism and Eastern Orthodoxy. Although it has retained much of the liturgy and the lines of authority of the Roman Catholic Church, it has embraced its own particular beliefs and practices regarding the Lord's Supper and the priesthood.

Of particular importance is the Anglican understanding of apostolic succession of bishops, which is also called the historic episcopate. Like the Roman Catholic and Eastern Orthodox Churches, Anglicans believe that their bishops maintain a direct and unbroken line of succession back to the original apostles. While the importance of apostolic succession is debated, Anglicans tend to consider it an asset because it gives the ordained ministry or priesthood a symbolic meaning and a dignified character. It also allows the Anglican Church to serve as a bridge between other Protestant denominations and the Roman Catholic and Eastern Orthodox Churches. In recent years, most Anglican churches have authorized the ordination of women as priests and bishops. The relationship between the Anglican Church and the Roman Catholic and Eastern Orthodox Churches has been disrupted because the Roman and Orthodox Churches resolutely deny the possibility of ordaining women into a ministry of apostolic succession. One of the reasons offered is that the apostles were male and their successors must be male also.

The role of bishops, or the episcopacy, is so impor-

tant in the Anglican church that many denominations, which are often organized along national boundaries, are called Episcopal: the Episcopal Church in the United States, the Scottish Episcopal Church. Most Anglican denominations use the word Anglican in their names, such as the Anglican Church of Canada. But some Anglican churches, such as the Church of Ireland and the Church of the Province of Central Africa, use neither *Anglican* nor *Episcopal* as part of their name.

Anglicans in North America

In 1578, the Church of England came to America with Sir Francis Drake and grew rapidly because of the missionary efforts of later explorers.

The Revolutionary War nearly destroyed the colonial Church of England. The church required that American priests be ordained in England, and many were unable to make the journey. When the war began, priests were forced to make a choice: They could take an oath of allegiance to the king and become Loyalists, then face persecution in America or escape to Canada. Or they could abandon their ties to England and remain committed to the American cause.

Following the war, there was no Church of England

Like the Roman Catholic and Eastern Orthodox Churches, Anglicans believe that their bishops maintain a direct and unbroken line of succession back to the original apostles.

in the United States, or so it appeared; but the church proved to be resilient. In 1783, the clergy in Connecticut elected Samuel Seabury as their prospective bishop. But the Church of England refused to consecrate him. He was finally consecrated in Scotland by bishops of the Scottish Episcopal Church. By 1787, the Archbishop of Canterbury consented to consecrate American bishops. And by 1789, the American churches had their own constitution, a revised *Book of Common Prayer,* and independence.

Even during the Civil War, when most other religious groups split over the issue of slavery, the Episcopal churches in America remained united. Thanks in part to a consistent pattern of unity, the Episcopal Church was able to establish seminaries, missionary agencies, institutions of learning, tract societies, and social programs.

Anglicanism arrived in Canada with the explorers of the 1600s and grew with immigrations from Europe and, during the Revolutionary War, from America. Canada was given its first bishop in 1787, and the church became independent of the Church of England about a century later.

Anglican and Episcopal Organization

In the Anglican and Episcopal Churches, the priest is vested with the pastoral oversight of the congregation. The priest is called a rector, which means ruler or vicar, a representative of the bishop. With the help of the vestry, the local administrative body, he or she administers the local affairs of the congregation. Churches, called parishes, are clustered in a regional diocese, under the spiritual and administrative leadership of an elected bishop. Each diocese is autonomous, but representatives from all the dioceses meet every three years to deliberate and to cooperate on common ministries and administration, such as denominational education, mission, communication, and stewardship, as well as social and financial programs.

Anglican and Episcopal Liturgy and Beliefs

The Anglican and Episcopal Churches are highly liturgical, profoundly influenced by *The Book of Common Prayer,* which contains the liturgy and prayers for both corporate and private worship.

The Lord's Supper is one of two sacraments that Jesus Christ commanded his followers to continue. The Anglican and Episcopal Churches and the Roman Catholic Church differ significantly in their understanding of Communion, particularly concerning the real or the symbolic presence of Christ in the bread and wine. Roman Catholics believe that when the elements are consecrated, they become the actual body and blood of Christ. Episcopalians believe that the elements exist together with the body and blood of Christ.

Lutherans generally accept the Anglican view, while many other Protestant churches understand that the bread and wine (or juice) are not changed at any point in the ritual. Rather, they are understood as symbols or signs that represent or point to the body and blood of Christ and that help us remember his sacrifice for the salvation of humanity. Anglicans and Episcopalians generally celebrate Holy Communion at each Sunday service.

Anglicans and Episcopalians also celebrate the sacrament of baptism for both infants and adults. Baptism can be administered by pouring, in which the water is poured, usually from a pitcher; by sprinkling, in which the priest dips his or her hand in the water and sprinkles it on the person's head; or by immersion, in which the whole person is submerged in the water. Many other Protestant denominations permit all three ways of administering baptism; others, especially the more conservative churches, require immersion.

In addition to baptism and Communion, Episcopalians, like Roman Catholics, recognize as sacraments confirmation, penance (confession and pardon), orders (ordination), marriage, and unction (prayers for healing). Sacraments other than baptism and Communion are commended by Scripture or tradition, but not by Jesus.

The liturgies of the Episcopal Church are either high or low. *High* refers to highly traditional, formalized worship. High church worship tends to involve the congregation's senses; priests use music, chimes or bells, incense, pageantry, and vestments (special clothing) to communicate and symbolize the meaning of the liturgy. Low church worship has a more evangelistic flavor and is more informal.

The Anglican and Episcopal Churches are credal churches; they accept both the Apostle's Creed and the Nicene Creed as the basis for belief. In addition, Anglicans and Episcopalians accept the Bible, the tradition of the church, and human reason as sources of authority for faith and life. John Wesley, founder of the Methodist Church, was an Anglican all his life and retained in his teachings the authority of Scripture, tradition, and reason, while adding the element of experience.

Anglican and Episcopal Membership in North America

The Episcopal Church in the United States has 2.5 million baptized members in over 7,300 parishes. The Anglican Church of Canada has about 850,000 baptized members in nearly 1,800 parishes.

For Further Reflection

Use the following questions and activities to reflect on the key points in the article.

THE LANGUAGE OF THE PRAYER BOOK

➤ Borrow from your pastor or from the church or community library several copies of *The Book of Common Prayer*.

➤ Tell the participants to read and compare the liturgies in contemporary and traditional language. Then discuss the following questions:

Which approach to the ritual seems most familiar? most effective? most rich in imagery? most faithful? (Be sure to ask the youth to explain their answers.)

THE CELEBRATION OF THE SACRAMENTS

➤ Invite the group to review the section "Anglican and Episcopal Liturgies and Beliefs."

➤ Explain or invite the pastor to explain the different understandings of Communion.

➤ Ask these questions:

What does your church believe about Communion? How does your church practice Communion?

If you are not Anglican or Episcopalian, in what ways is Communion in your church like that of the Anglican and Episcopal Churches? How is it different?

What does Communion mean to you? In what ways do you recognize the presence of Christ in Communion?

➤ Ask these questions about the other sacraments:

Does your church consider baptism a sacrament? Are confirmation, penance (confession and pardon), orders (ordination), marriage, and unction (prayers for healing) regarded as sacraments? as ordinances? as ways in which God is revealed? as special ways of worshiping?

What do confirmation, penance, orders, and so on mean in your church? What do they mean to you?

EPISCOPALIAN WORSHIP

➤ Invite discussion of worship in high and low churches. If possible, visit a worship service at an Anglican or Episcopal church or ask a priest for copies of the order of worship. Have available a copy of *The Book of Common Prayer*.

➤ Ask the participants to compare and contrast the high or low worship service in the Anglican or Episcopal Church with the worship of their congregation. Then discuss these questions:

What sights, sounds, and smells did (would) you notice in the Anglican or Episcopal service? How did (would) they affect your understanding of worship? How did (would) they affect your participation in the service?

If your church's worship were more like the Anglican or Episcopal service, how would it affect your congregation? Why?

Friends: The Quakers

The Quakers prefer to be called Friends. They received the nickname Quakers from an early leader's encouragement to quake, or tremble, at the word of God. Quakers did not originate in North America; the religious group was founded in England, by George Fox, in 1647-1648. The Friends were persecuted because they refused to support and attend the established Church of England and also because they refused to grant civil authorities the power they claimed. Many of them decided to seek religious freedom in the new American colonies. They were disappointed; when they arrived in Massachusetts, the Puritans, or Congregationalists, persecuted them as well. Finally, a number of Friends settled in Pennsylvania where they found peace. Pennsylvania was named for William Penn, a Friend, and is sometimes called the Quaker State.

Simplicity governed all aspects of Friends' lives. Dress, language, and lifestyle were to be modest in all respects. The group abstained from alcohol, tobacco, and worldly amusements. Friends refused to participate in war, including the suppression of the Native Americans, with whom they enjoyed cordial relations. Today, the Friends are probably best known for their continuing stance against war and participation in war.

Friends believe that each person has an inner light, an inner spirituality given by God. Each person's goal is to listen to God's Spirit and to work toward perfection in this life. While there are both conservative and liberal interpretations of the tradition, most Friends would agree that the fundamental goodness of humanity is to be cherished and developed.

Friends' worship varies from denomination to denomination, but the classic style is a Quaker meeting. Friends' congregations are called meetings, and the buildings in which they worship are called meeting houses. In a Quaker meeting, Friends sit silently waiting for the Spirit of God to inspire or give insight to a member of the meeting; then he or she will tell the group what he or she has been inspired to say. The ideal of the meeting is to reach harmony in worship and consensus in decision-making through the practice of quiet reflection. Other Friends' worship, such as that of the Evangelical Friends, resembles standard Protestant services. Friends do not observe baptism or Communion.

Government is strictly congregational, though most meetings are affiliated with others in national denominations; the Friends United Meeting, with 50,000 members, and the General Conference of the Religious Society of Friends, with 32,000 members, are the largest denominations. The Canadian Yearly Meeting of the Religious Society of Friends is affiliated with both of the major denominations in the United States. It represents over 1,000 members in Canada in 20 meetings.

For Further Reflection

Use the following questions and activities to reflect on the key points in the article.

SIMPLICITY

Quakers dress, speak, and act simply. What does simplicity mean to you?

How would your life be different if you were modest or abstinent in your participation in worldly amusements?

Do you think abstinence from tobacco and alcohol is good? Is it a spiritual exercise? Why? Why not?

WORSHIP

Quakers usually worship in a meeting, in which any or all of the people may receive insight from God and speak. They do not have a preacher, a choir, or established ways for the congregation to participate.

How is Quaker worship similar to worship in your church? How is it different?

What is your goal for the time you spend in worship? What is the goal of your congregation or meeting? Why is it difficult to think about the goals of worship?

In what ways would worshiping in silence change or improve your personal worship experience?

Methodist Churches

Most Methodists in the United States belong to The United Methodist Church and are therefore properly described as United Methodists. But there are other Methodist and related churches, some of which use the term *Methodist* while others, like the Church of the Nazarene, do not. Some of the churches are described as Wesleyan, a reference to John Wesley, the founder of the Methodist movement. In some countries, the Methodist churches have merged with other denominations to form united churches, such as the United Church of Canada. The term *Methodist* refers to the entire tradition. Each denomination within the tradition has its own title: United Methodist, Free Methodist, and so on.

The family of churches called Methodists is distinct from other Christians partly because of its roots in the English culture of the 1700s. At that time, the Church of England (see "Anglican Churches," beginning on page 86) had grown away from the common people, who were victims of poverty and corruption.

John Wesley was born in Epworth, England in 1703. He was so deeply religious, disciplined, and methodical in his spiritual and practical life that in his youth, he earned the nickname that would identify a tradition in the Christian church: Methodist.

Wesley was ordained a priest in the Church of England and engaged in an active ministry. After he returned from a depressing and ill-fated trip to the colony of Georgia, Wesley had a profound spiritual experience that brought to him a deep assurance of salvation by and in Christ. The experience brought new zeal to his commitment to Christ.

The excitement and vitality of Wesley's preaching offended staid and formal church officials, and soon John Wesley was kept from preaching in church pulpits. He began to preach outside in streets and fields, where thousands of commoners heard the good news of Jesus Christ.

The people, many of whom stood outside the ministry of the Anglican church, hungered for more. Wesley organized them into small clusters, called classes and societies, for the purpose of study, prayer, and spiritual support. Lay groups remain a vital part of ministry in the Methodist tradition.

Circuits Grow in the Colonies

Wesley's ministry moved to the American colonies in 1760, under the leadership of Philip Embury and his cousin Barbara Heck in New York and Robert Strawbridge in Pennsylvania, Maryland, Delaware, and Virginia.

Wesley realized that the Methodist societies in America needed more leadership. At what has since been called the Christmas Conference, Richard Whatcoat, Thomas Vasey, and Thomas Coke, who had been sent by Wesley, convened a meeting of all the preachers in the colonies. On December 24, 1784 at Lovely Lane Chapel in Baltimore, Maryland, sixty preachers met. They elected and ordained Francis Asbury as the first bishop, and they formally organized the Methodist Episcopal Church.

Meanwhile . . .

The United Brethren were growing under the leadership of Philip William Otterbein and Martin Boehm. Otterbein was a German Reformed pastor who was favorably influenced by the Wesleyan movement. He was a close friend of Francis Asbury. Boehm was a Mennonite preacher who had been expelled from the Mennonite communion because of his preaching style. During a chance meeting, Otterbein heard Boehm preach and responded by declaring, "We are brethren!" The United Brethren Church was begun. The United Brethren and the Methodist Church had beliefs and practices in common. But Methodist services were in English, while the Brethren worshiped in German.

Jacob Albright, a Lutheran pastor, had fallen into a deep depression when his young children died. He attended a Methodist class meeting and had a heartwarming experience that gave him new assurance of his relationship to God. He began preaching with renewed vigor and joy. Eventually, people who heard him preach banded together to become the Evangelical Association.

African Churches Develop

In 1816, The African Methodist Episcopal Church was formally organized by Blacks who wanted freedom from mistreatment by white Methodists. Richard Allen and Daniel Coker were instrumental in the growth of The African Methodist Episcopal Church.

In 1822, the African Methodist Episcopal, Zion, Church was established. This group was built by and for worshipers of African descent who had been members of the John Street Church in New York City.

In 1870, five years after the Civil War, The Christian Methodist Episcopal Church, was formed by African Americans in the South.

Methodist Government

Virtually all Methodist or Methodist-related denominations are connectional, which means that congregations are not independent, but cooperate nationally and internationally to advance the work of the whole church. Local churches are under the care of elders or deacons who are responsible to district superintendents and bishops. In some Methodist-related traditions, there are general superintendents rather than bishops.

Methodist Beliefs

In the Methodist tradition, the range of theological beliefs is diverse. Methodist, Methodist-related churches, and most other Protestant denominations have in common the conviction that God is merciful and loving; that God is three-in-one (God, Christ, and the Holy Spirit are one God, yet distinct); and that there are two sacraments, baptism and Communion.

The Methodist tradition emphasizes an understanding of God's grace, which is evident in our lives in three ways. *Prevenient grace* is the love of God that surrounds all of humanity, even before we are aware of God. Prevenient grace prompts people to turn toward God and to repent of sin. Through God's *justifying grace*, people truly repent, change, and are transformed by God's forgiveness into what the Bible calls a new creation. In new birth, God's *sanctifying grace* draws us toward Christian perfection, which Wesley described as being filled with the love of God. Some Methodist and Methodist-related groups emphasize sanctifying grace. These groups are known as Holiness churches. The Church of the Nazarene, the Free Methodist Church, and the Wesleyan Church are holiness churches.

Methodists, to one degree or another, are known for their willingness to understand and accept differences in points of view and in theology. While there is a diversity of belief within the tradition, Methodist Christians rely on Scripture, tradition, reason, and experience as sources of authority in matters of faith and practice. Some Methodist-related groups, such as the Nazarenes and Wesleyans, tend to emphasize Scripture and experience and to attach less importance to tradition and reason.

Scripture: The Bible is the record of God's acts in Creation and in life. Scripture is the most important source of guidance for the Christian life.

Tradition: The community of faith checks and reexamines its traditions by returning to Scripture. The people called Methodist look at the history and practice of the church and at the biblical message in light of modern experience.

Reason: Methodists believe that God has given people the capacity to think and that their minds are an asset in formulating and affirming their religious beliefs.

Experience: Methodists respect the spiritual experience of individuals and congregations and recognize that experience can convey new insight into the will of God. Methodist Christians believe in regular prayer, devotion, and Scripture reading.

The United Methodist Church

The United Methodist Church is the largest Methodist church in the world and the second largest Protestant denomination in the United States. (Not all United Methodist congregations are in the United States.) There are just under 9 million United Methodists in 37,000 local churches. The United Methodist Church was formed in 1968 with the merger of The Methodist Church and the Evangelical United Brethren Church. The denomination is connectional, organized into charges (local churches or circuits), districts, conferences, jurisdictions, and the general church. The United Methodist Church also has a strong episcopacy; bishops, individually and collectively, are responsible for the spiritual and administrative affairs of the denomination. Unlike most Protestant denominations, the bishops appoint pastors to local churches. (Most Protestant churches call or elect their pastors.)

African Methodist Churches

The African Methodist Episcopal Church has 3.5 million members in 8,000 local churches. The African Methodist Episcopal Church, Zion has 1.2 million in 3,000 local churches. The Christian Methodist Episcopal Church has more than 700,000 members in over 2,300 local churches. The historically Black churches also have a strong episcopacy.

Other Methodist and Methodist Related Denominations in North America

A number of other denominations fall within the Methodist tradition. Three in the United States and Canada are holiness churches: The Free Methodist Church of North America, the Church of the Nazarene, and the Wesleyan Church. All three denominations began in Methodist churches. The Free Methodist Church maintains an episcopacy; the other two use a system of superintendents.

Adapted from "Families of Faith: United Methodists," by Micheal Selleck, *The Magazine for Christian Youth!*, October 1992 © Copyright 1992 by Cokesbury.

For Further Reflection

Use the following questions and activities to reflect on the key points in the article.

SOURCES OF AUTHORITY

➤ Divide the class into four groups and give each group Bibles and a concordance.

➤ Invite the groups to investigate the sources of authority accepted by Methodist Churches. Assign each group one source of authority: Scripture, tradition, reason, or experience. Ask the members of the group to consider an issue from the point of view they have been assigned—for example, they may consider the question, What does the Scripture say about the issue?

Select an issue, such as the authority of women, the interpretation of Scripture (Is it literal? figurative? open to individual interpretation?), or the practice of baptism. Or ask the youth to consider issues that are important in today's culture: abuse, addiction, sexual orientation or behavior.

As an alternative, assign each group an issue and ask the members of the group to consider the issue from all four points of view: Scripture, tradition, reason, and experience.

➤ Bring the groups together to discuss these questions:

What about the issue did you understand in new ways because you looked at it from the perspective of Scripture? tradition? reason? experience?

What new insights did you gain? What questions did you consider that hadn't occurred to you before?

Did thinking about the issue from several points of view help your understanding of the issue? Why? Why not?

Have you learned a helpful way of thinking about issues? Why? Why not?

GOD'S GRACE

➤ Invite the participants to review the information about three different expressions of grace. Ask each person to explain the meaning of prevenient, justifying, and sanctifying grace.

➤ Write on a large sheet of paper brief definitions based on the participants' explanations. Ask the youth to compare and contrast the definitions.

➤ Then discuss these questions:

What is your understanding of grace?

When have you experienced God's grace? What was it like?

Do you feel as if you are surrounded by God's grace even when you are not aware of it? Why? Why not?

What would help you to recognize God's grace?

Baptist Churches

Of all the families of Protestantism, Baptists are the most problematic to describe because Baptists consider each local church an autonomous unit and because there is a diversity of Baptist congregations and Baptist organizations.

History

Some Baptists believe that the Baptist Church has no founder but Christ and that Baptists have been preaching and practicing the faith since the days of John the Baptist. However, Baptist churches as we know them first appeared in Holland and England in the early 1600s. Even then, there were many different churches in the Baptist family. The Pedobaptists baptized children (*pedo* means child). The Antipedobaptists, who thought that infant baptism was unscriptural, rebaptized adults who had been baptized as infants. (Sometimes Antipedobaptists were described as Anabaptists [*ana* means redo], but the term Anabaptist ordinarily refers to a group with a different tradition and history.)

Many Baptists fled to England because of persecution, largely at the hands of continental European Protestants, and merged with early English separatists. Together they established the roots of modern Baptist churches. Many later fled from England because of religious persecution.

The Baptists came to America around 1640. By the end of the eighteenth century, Baptist churches were well established in North America; but they were not as well structured or as effective as most other Protestant churches. Issues for Baptists concerned church structure—whether Baptist congregations should be united in any way—and the relationship of church and society.

Different Churches

There are probably more than thirty Baptist denominations in the United States. (No one knows an exact number of denominations; new ones are created regularly.) Together they have about 100,000 local churches and a combined enrollment of over 30 million members. Baptist churches are independent of one another, but many are bound together by their allegiance to particular principles and doctrines. Many congregations are connected to one another through associations and conventions so that they can minister more effectively; they combine their efforts in areas such as curriculum development, education, and missionary support and development. It is not unusual to find local Baptist churches affiliating with more than one cooperative organization—for instance, a local Baptist congregation may belong to the American Baptist Churches in

Baptists believe in the inspiration of the Bible and in its trustworthiness as the sole rule of life.

the United States of America; the National Baptist Convention, USA, Inc.; and the Southern Baptist Convention.

Different Beliefs and Practices

Although Baptist belief and theology covers a lot of ground, there are core principles of faith that are held by most Baptists.

■ Baptists believe in the inspiration of the Bible and in its trustworthiness as the sole rule of life. Conservative Baptists adhere to the literal truth of the Bible, while moderates believe that the Scriptures are open to personal interpretation and that some passages in the Bible may be symbolic.

■ Baptists confess Jesus Christ as the Lord of life.

■ Baptists affirm the right and freedom of every individual to approach God without an intermediary, such as a priest.

■ With other Protestant denominations, Baptists believe that salvation is the province of God. We are saved by God's grace and by the power of the Holy Spirit and not by any merit of our own.

■ Baptists practice both baptism and Holy Communion, but many consider them ordinances, commands of Christ, rather than sacraments. Today, virtually all Baptists would be considered Antipedobaptists because they regard infant baptism as unscriptural. Baptism by immersion takes place when the individual accepts the lordship of Jesus Christ.

■ Baptist theology says that all people stand in need of redemption from sin and that redemption is possible through the law of God and through the expectation of God's final triumph over the power of sin.

Baptists also have in common principles about Christian life and practice. Moderates tend to accept the prevailing interpretation of the separation of church and state, while conservatives favor prayer in public schools. Moderate churches allow women to hold church offices; some will even ordain women. Conservatives often oppose women in positions of authority.

Southern Baptist Convention

With over 15 million members in more than 38,000 congregations, the Southern Baptist Convention is the largest fellowship of Baptist churches. It is also the largest Protestant denomination in the United States.

The Southern Baptist Convention was formed in 1845 before the Civil War. Like Presbyterians and Methodists in the South, southern Baptists disagreed with their northern counterparts and elected to go their own way. Slavery was one of the issues that split the church. Today, the Southern Baptist Convention is a national body with churches all over the United States.

Moderates and conservatives coexist within the denomination, but diverge significantly in matters of doctrine and practice. Most of the leadership in the convention is currently held by conservative Baptists. More moderate members, rather than going through denominational channels, have created a parallel organization, called the Cooperative Baptist Fellowship, as a channel for developing resources and for directing energy into mission.

Southern Baptist churches are autonomous. They are grouped into regional associations and state conventions. The Southern Baptist Convention is the national church organization to which local churches send messengers.

National Baptist Convention of America and National Baptist Convention, USA, Inc.

The first Baptist church for African Americans was organized in Augusta, Georgia in 1773. Before the Civil War, slaves usually assembled in their own churches, often with the blessing and assistance of their white owners. After Nat Turner's slave revolt in 1831, laws in some sections of the country kept African Americans from assembling for any reason. After the Civil War, black congregations grew rapidly. Historically, the majority of African American Christians have been either Baptist or Methodist.

Several black Baptist churches tried to form associations. The National Baptist Convention of America was formed in Atlanta in 1895. In 1915, the church split over issues of adopting a charter or plan of organization. Congregations that preferred not to adopt the charter became the National Baptist Convention of America, which is sometimes referred to as unincorporated. It has 3.5 million members. Congregations that adopted the charter became the National Baptist Convention of the United States of

> Baptist theology says that all people stand in need of redemption from sin and that redemption is possible through the law of God and through the expectation of God's final triumph over the power of sin.

America, Inc., which has more than 8 million members in 33,000 congregations. It is the largest historically-black, voluntary organization in the world.

American Baptist Churches in the United States of America

This is a cooperative organization of Baptist congregations. It was founded in 1907 and has about 1.5 million members in nearly 6,000 congregations. In 1950, it changed its name from The Northern Baptist Convention to the American Baptist Convention; and in 1972, it was renamed the American Baptist Churches in the United States of America. Most American Baptist churches were congregations that did not become a part of the Southern Baptist Convention when it was organized in 1845. Members of the American Baptist Church tend to be more liberal than members of the Southern Baptist Convention, especially regarding ecumenical endeavors.

Baptists in Canada

There are fewer Baptists in Canada than in the United States. Most Baptist organizations in the United States are also represented in Canada, but Canadian Baptists also have a unique history. The largest organization of Baptist congregations is the Canadian Baptist Federation, which represents 131,000 members in 1,100 congregations.

Adapted from "Families of Faith: Baptists," by Ed Trimmer; *The Magazine for Christian Youth!*, December 1991; copyright © 1991 by Cokesbury.

For Further Reflection

Use the following questions and activities to reflect on the key points in the article.

➤ Invite the participants to review "Different Beliefs and Practices." Provide a Bible for each person and a topical concordance for each small group. Have available a one-volume commentary and a Bible dictionary.

➤ Ask the participants to form groups of three or four people. Assign the members of each group a doctrinal issue, and tell them to research the issue and to discuss the questions. Then bring the groups together to report.

GROUP 1:
INSPIRATION OF THE BIBLE

What Bible passages mention the authority of Scripture? (Tell the group to look up the word *Scripture* in the concordance and to look for cross-references if necessary.)

What does the Bible say about the authority of Scripture?

What is your understanding of Scripture? Do you regard it as a source of authority in what you believe and do? Do you believe that it is literally true? inspired by God? written by people of faith? Why?

GROUP 2:
APPROACHING GOD PERSONALLY

What Bible passages mention the ways we are invited or required to approach God? (Tell the group to look up *worship, prayer, God's call,* or *God's voice* in the concordance.)

What does the Scripture tell us about approaching God?

How do you approach God? (Invite members of the group to tell a brief story about their experience of God.)

GROUP 3:
BELIEVER'S BAPTISM

What Scripture references mention baptism?

What practice(s) do they describe?

In the Scripture, was anyone baptized who did not make a personal confession of faith?

What is the practice of baptism in your church? (Invite the participants to tell what they know about their own baptism.)

Are people who have not made a confession of faith baptized in your church?

GROUP 4:
THE AUTHORITY AND ROLE OF WOMEN

How many passages can you find in which women are told that they have little or no authority?

How many passages show women in positions of leadership? (Suggest that the participants look up the names of people Paul greeted at the end of his letters.)

Does your church ordain women? allow women to hold office?

What do you believe about the ordination of women? Why?

Mennonite Churches

Mennonite and Baptist churches both have roots in the Anabaptist, or rebaptizing, tradition. Anabaptists who lived in Central and Eastern Europe later moved to North America and became known as Mennonites.

Mennonite Roots

Menno Simons was a sixteenth-century Dutch Roman Catholic priest. He was converted during the Protestant Reformation. Simons rejected not only the practices of the Roman Catholic Church, but also the government-sponsored Protestant churches that stood in the traditions of Luther, Zwingli, and Calvin. Simons helped to organize so many congregations of like-minded people that they became known as Mennonites.

In 1525 in Zurich, Switzerland, people who objected to the reforms of Ulrich Zwingli established the first known Mennonite congregation. Because Mennonites rejected any partnership between church and state, they encountered opposition from reformed congregations in four countries. Unwelcome in Germany, Switzerland, Holland, and England, they eventually looked for a home in the new American colonies.

The first American Mennonite congregation was founded by German immigrants in Pennsylvania in 1683. Immigrants from Germany and Switzerland and later from Russia and Poland established Mennonite communities in Pennsylvania, Ohio, Virginia, Indiana, Illinois, and Canada.

Baptism and the Lord's Supper

Menno Simons and his followers believed that individuals baptized as infants must be rebaptized as adult believers. In Mennonite churches, baptism and the Lord's Supper are observed as ordinances, or commands; but they are not considered sacraments. Baptism is understood as a public testimony of faith, and Communion is an expression of fellowship and unity in Christ. Foot-washing generally accompanies Communion.

Mennonite Doctrine

Mennonite belief is based on a confession of faith signed in 1682 in Holland. The confession affirms that God is Creator and that Jesus Christ is the Son of God and our Redeemer. Christ restores fallen humanity, although individuals must still repent of sin and be converted in order to attain salvation. Mennonites believe in eternal reward for the faithful and punishment for the wicked. The law of Christ in the gospel forms the basis of belief and practice.

Mennonites emphasize Christian living based on Scripture. While different Mennonite groups vary in their application of historic Mennonite practices, they generally prefer to marry among themselves, among the "spiritually kindred," and usually refuse to bear arms or to serve in the military. Mennonites are pacifists, and their churches are sometimes called peace churches. Some strict Mennonites refuse to take an oath in a court of law, to hold public office, or to vote in public elections.

Many Mennonites dress "plain." The Amish, who represent a conservative movement within the Mennonite tradition, have an especially strict dress code.

Mennonite Denominations

The Mennonite Church has nearly 100,000 members in over 1,000 congregations in the United States and nearly 15,000 members in over 100 congregations in Canada. It is the largest organized body of Mennonites in North America. The General Conference Mennonite Church represents a wide variety of ethnic communities, primarily immigrants from Western and Eastern Europe. There are almost 34,000 General Conference Mennonites in more than 200 congregations in the United States. The Mennonite Church and the General Conference Mennonite Church are considering the possibility of union.

Congregations in the Old Order Amish Church hold to a conservative interpretation of the Mennonite tradition. Its churches are not organized into conventions or conferences. The Old Order Amish Church has 77,000 members in nearly 900 congregations in the United States and 17 congregations in Canada. The Conference of Mennonites in Canada originated in Russia and dates from the beginning of the twentieth century. It has 37,000 members in approximately 150 congregations.

For Further Reflection

Use the following questions to reflect on the key points in the article.

Does your congregation rebaptize? Why? Why not?

What is your congregation's understanding of baptism?

How is Communion practiced in your congregation? What does it mean? In what ways does it demonstrate unity in Christ?

Does your congregation practice footwashing? Read **John 13:1-16**. What is the significance of footwashing?

What does your church teach about eternal rewards and punishments? What do you think?

Is your church a peace church? Why? Why not?

Christian Church (Disciples of Christ), Christian Churches, and Churches of Christ

The tradition that includes the Christian Church (Disciples of Christ), the Christian Churches, and the Churches of Christ is sometimes called the Restoration Movement because of its emphasis on restoring New Testament Christianity. The tradition is unique to the United States, although it has a small following in Canada as well. The four founding fathers, who took the religion to the frontier, were originally Presbyterian; they were Barton Stone, Thomas and Alexander Campbell (father and son), and Walter Scott. All four agreed that the primary task of Christian faith was unity in Christ and with one another.

A Convergence of Opinion

The founders of the Disciples of Christ, Christian Churches, and Churches of Christ thought that creeds were not only unnecessary, but divisive. They held that there was no creed but Christ. Since the task of faith is unity with Christ and among believers, whatever divides people—such as opinions about administration, clergy titles, or other human inventions—should be avoided. Barton Stone and the Campbells had trouble with established congregations because of differences of opinion. They ultimately left their churches and took with them groups of followers. Stone's new congregation took the name *Christian*.

Alexander Campbell left Scotland to join Thomas in Pennsylvania. He brought with him the concept of free congregations, which would be independent from one another and at liberty to follow their own simple faith in Jesus Christ as Son of God and Messiah. He felt that creeds, titles, and clerical authority had no justification in Scripture. Father and son joined forces, using the name *Disciples* for their followers. In 1832, they merged with the Christian Church to form the Christian Church (Disciples of Christ), although local churches retained the freedom to keep their own designations.

Organization

In the Christian tradition, the local congregation is of primary importance. Only the Christian Church (Disciples of Christ) has become an organized denomination. Since 1968, the Christian Church (Disciples of Christ) has had

The founders of the Disciples of Christ, Christian Churches, and Churches of Christ thought that creeds were not only unnecessary, but divisive. They held that there was no creed but Christ.

three levels of representational government: local, regional, and national. Congregations are the principle unit of government. Each local church calls its own pastor, sets its own budget, oversees its own ministry, and elects representatives to the regional and national assemblies.

On the national level, Disciples meet to plan, implement, and oversee the denomination's ministries. Regional matters concern the selection, education, training, and ordination of clergy, as well as counsel and assistance for local churches.

Some of the Christian Churches are involved cooperatively through regional bodies known as conventions, but some are not. The Churches of Christ fiercely resist any notion of denominational entanglement, although some of them cooperate with other congregations to operate schools, children's homes, and evangelistic campaigns. In some quarters, even cooperative missions are controversial.

In Matters of Faith

Churches in the Christian tradition adhere to core beliefs about God, Christ, and the Bible. In some churches, individual interpretation and conscience are allowed and encouraged. The tradition holds that salvation is through the sacrifice of Christ and that all people are in need of redemption from their sinful nature. Disciples do not accept a fixed catechism or set of teachings; faith in Jesus Christ is decisive. Baptism is for adult believers, and Communion is observed every Sunday.

Faith and Belief: Differences

In most matters of faith and belief, Christian Churches and Churches of Christ are in accord with the Disciples of Christ. They are, however, generally more strict, conservative, even fundamentalist. Some Churches of Christ believe that ordinances should be observed in ways initiated by the earliest apostles. The most conservative do not use instrumental music in their services, although they may sing. Many do not observe holidays, such as Christmas, claiming that holiday observances are not commanded by Scripture. Except in the Christian Church (Disciples of Christ), women are not allowed to be leaders such as deacons, elders, or ministers.

Christian Church (Disciples of Christ)

The Christian Church (Disciples of Christ) has approximately one million members, known as Disciples, in nearly 4,000 congregations in the United States. In Canada, there are 4,000 Disciples in thirty-five congregations.

Christian Churches and Churches of Christ

Christian Churches and Churches of Christ do not maintain denominational statistics. In the United States, there are an estimated one million members in over 5,000 congregations. In Canada, there are an estimated 7,500 members in 1,500 congregations.

For Further Reflection

Use the following questions and activities to reflect on the key points in the article.

CHRISTIAN UNITY

➤ Give each person a Bible. Have available a topical concordance and one or two one-volume commentaries. Ask everyone to find two passages that encourage unity in Jesus Christ. (Divide a large group into teams.)

➤ Bring the participants together to talk about the Scripture. Ask these questions:

What is the passage you found? What does it say about Christian unity?

Is the Scripture enough to hold people together in Christ, or is church organization necessary? Why?

The four founders thought that creeds and human lines of authority created unnecessary division among Christians. What do you think? Why?

CHRISTIAN CHURCH (DISCIPLES OF CHRIST)

➤ Tell the group that Disciples believe in individual freedom to interpret the Scripture. Discuss these questions:

How much freedom does your denomination allow for individual interpretation?

How much freedom do you think is OK? Why?

How do you know when a passage is figurative and when it should be taken literally or at face value?

When people disagree about what the Bible actually says, whom should you believe?

Do you understand what you read in the Bible without an explanation or interpretation?

How do you learn what the Bible means?

CHRISTIAN CHURCHES AND CHURCHES OF CHRIST

➤ Give each person a Bible. Have available topical concordances and a Bible dictionary. Ask the participants to research and discuss these issues:

How should we observe ordinances of the church?

How did believers in the early church practice the faith in worship? sacraments? their life together? (See **Acts 2** and a Bible dictionary.)

Can we practice the faith as early Christians did? Why? Why not?

Does the passage of time make a difference in Christian faith and practice? Why? Why not?

What passages mention the use of musical instruments? Does the Scripture refer to musical instruments used in worship? Does your church use instruments in worship? How do you feel about using musical instruments in worship?

What passages mention celebrations? Do you think celebrating holidays is idolatry? Why? Why not?

Pentecostal Churches

Pentecostals get their name from the experience of Pentecost when the Holy Spirit descended on the disciples (**Acts 2**).

Pentecostals believe that a person who has been baptized by the Holy Spirit will ordinarily manifest one or more spiritual gifts, such as those recorded in **1 Corinthians 12 and 14**: wisdom, knowledge, faith, healing, miracles, prophecy, discernment of false spirits, unknown tongues, and interpretation of tongues. Many Pentecostal churches emphasize the gift of *glossolalia,* or speaking in tongues.

Tongues can be either a divine language, known only to God, or a foreign language that the speaker has not learned but speaks only by the inspiration of the Holy Spirit. The sign of speaking in tongues is considered by many Pentecostal churches to be normative; that is, if a Christian has been baptized by the Holy Spirit, he or she will speak in tongues.

History

Pentecostalism began in the Holiness movement of the late 1800s and in the Azusa Street Revival, which took place in Los Angeles in 1906. William J. Seymour, an African American preacher who was influenced by a Methodist and holiness upbringing and by the teachings of Charles Fox Parham, founded the Apostolic Faith Gospel Mission in an abandoned Methodist church on Azusa Street. The revival started when several African American Christians gathered to seek the baptism of the Holy Spirit. For the next three years, meetings were held every day, usually all day, and attracted people from all over the country. The services of the Azusa Street Revival were interracial, which was unusual in the early 1900s. Many of the gifts of the Spirit, including the gift of tongues, were evident during the revival. One result of early Pentecostalism was that speaking in tongues became a part of worship and personal devotions in many communities. Another unusual result was the participation of women in public activities.

The Azusa Street church hosted thousands of visitors from the United States and from many other countries. They returned to their homes and to their home churches and lit the spark of pentecostal worship there. Pentecostal congregations and denominations have been formed in communities around the world. Pentecostals are also members of mainline Protestant denominations and the Roman Catholic Church. Technically, people who practice Pentecostalism in non-Pentecostal churches are neo-Pentecostals, but they are usually referred to as charis-matics. (*Charismatic* comes from the Greek word for gifts.) Some traditional Pentecostals now describe themselves as charismatics.

Denominations

Four of the six largest Pentecostal denominations were organized shortly before World War I. (Many Pentecostal churches do not keep or issue statistical reports, so the size of some of the denominations is estimated.) The Assemblies of God has about 2.6 million members in 12,000 congregations; it was formed from smaller groups in 1914. The Pentecostal Holiness Church, International, has 150,000 members and began with the merger, in 1911, of the Fire-Baptized Holiness Church and the Pentecostal Holiness Church. The Church of God (Cleveland, Tennessee) has about 675,000 members and was organized in 1902. The Church of God in Christ, a historically black denomination has 5.5 million members in 15,000 congregations. It was started in 1897 in the Memphis, Tennessee area.

Three other Pentecostal denominations have memberships of a significant size. The International Church of the Foursquare Gospel has 200,000 members in 1,600 congregations; it was founded in 1927 by Aimee Semple McPherson, a flamboyant faith healer who toured the country preaching and healing. Several groups broke away from the Assemblies of God in 1916 and came together in 1945 to form the United Pentecostal Church International; it has about 550,000 members in 3,700 congregations. The Pentecostal Assemblies of Canada, which have 195,000 members in 1,000 congregations, were incorporated in 1919 and are directly related to the Assemblies of God denomination in the United States.

Doctrines and Beliefs

One of the most significant doctrinal issues among Pentecostal denominations concerns the manifestation of Christian experience. Some Pentecostal denominations teach that Christian experience involves (1) conversion, (2) sanctification, and (3) baptism by the Holy Spirit, with the evidence of tongues. Denominations that teach the three stages of Christian experience, such as the Church of God (Cleveland, Tennessee) and the Church of God in Christ, have theological roots in the Wesleyan tradition, with its emphasis on sanctification.

Other Pentecostal denominations, such as The Assemblies of God and the International Church of the Foursquare Gospel, understand sanctification as a process that begins at conversion, but is not completed or perfected until death. They understand Christian experience as (1) conversion and (2) baptism in the Holy Spirit, with the evidence of tongues. A third way of understanding Christian experience was formulated in 1913 during a dispute over the baptismal formula. The question raised was, Should people be baptized in the name of Jesus or in the name of the Father, Son, and Holy Spirit? Believers who thought that people should be baptized only in the name of Jesus formed several small denominations and, in 1945, the United Pentecostal Church, International. Most Pentecostals believe that Scripture is divinely inspired and literally infallible. Most teach premillenialism, the belief that Christ will come a second time immediately before a thousand year period of holiness, in which he will rule the world (**Revelation 20:1-5**).

Many Pentecostal denominations believe in and practice faith healing. Their positions on issues such as divorce, abortion, and the rights of women are usually conservative. During World War I, most Pentecostal denominations were pacifist; now most are ardent supporters of a strong military.

Worship

Worship in Pentecostal churches is usually informal. Formal ritual is frowned on as the form rather than the reality of religion and as a deterrent to the working of the Spirit. Generally services include public and private prayer; congregational singing and special singing; preaching; a time for the gifts of the Spirit, including glossolalia; and an altar call.

Most Pentecostal denominations recognize two sacraments or ordinances: baptism, usually by immersion; and the Lord's Supper. Some denominations have given special status to other rituals such as foot-washing and divine healing.

Pentecostal beliefs have influenced many churches through the charismatic movement in the 1970s and through the development of a deeper spirituality for individual church members. The enthusiasm of some Pentecostals has been tempered over the years, but the worship of most Pentecostal churches is still filled with emotion.

For Further Reflection

Use the following questions and activities to reflect on the key points in the article.

GLOSSOLALIA

➤ Invite the group to review the information on glossolalia, or speaking in tongues. Ask the participants to form small groups. Distribute Bibles, and ask each group to read one of these Scriptures: **Acts 2; 1 Corinthians 12, 13, 14**. Then ask these questions:

What does the Bible say about the gifts of the Holy Spirit? about the gift of tongues?

What qualifications does the Scripture set on the gift of tongues? on all spiritual gifts?

How does your denomination understand the gifts of the Holy Spirit?

DOCTRINES, BELIEF, AND WORSHIP

➤ Ask the participants to review the information about Pentecostals' doctrines and beliefs. Tell the youth to look up **Revelation 20:1-20** and to use a commentary or Bible dictionary to help them understand the Scripture. Then discuss these questions:

How does your church talk about Christian experience? Does your denomination understand Christian experience as three-stage or two-stage process? Does Christian experience and baptism involve Jesus only or the whole Trinity? In what ways are the beliefs of your denomination like the Pentecostals'? How are they different?

What does your church teach about the Bible? What do you believe about the Bible? Is it divinely inspired? literally infallible? Why? Why not?

What is premillenialism? What does your denomination teach about the final coming of Christ?

Does anyone know what will happen or when Christ will come? What does the second coming of Christ mean to you?

➤ Discuss Pentecostal worship using these questions:

What is the worship service like in your church? Is it spontaneous? formal?

If the ritual or liturgy is formal, is the Holy Spirit present? Why? Why not?

Is a formal worship service religion without reality? Why? Why not? What makes religion and worship real for you? Why?

Other North American Traditions

Many Christian traditions have been established in the United States and Canada. A number of religious groups are unconventional; they don't fall into the categories of Roman Catholic, Eastern Orthodox, or Protestant. But they have influenced religious development in North America.

The Mormon Tabernacle on Temple Square, Salt Lake City, Utah. Photo courtesy of The Salt Lake Convention and Visitors Bureau

Christian Science

> The essential doctrine
> of Christian Science
> is that
> God is mind.
> As an all-knowing,
> loving, and compassionate
> father and mother,
> God only wants
> what is best for
> God's children.
> Illness,
> financial problems,
> and unhappiness
> are not God's will.

In the late 1800s, Mary Baker Eddy worked out principles of healing based on theology and spirituality. She wrote about her work in a textbook, *Science and Health with Keys to the Scriptures*, which she hoped would be used for the purpose of reinstating the lost art of Christian healing. Her teaching is essential to the beliefs of the Church of Christ, Scientist.

The essential doctrine of Christian Science is that God is mind. As an all-knowing, loving, and compassionate father and mother, God only wants what is best for God's children. Illness, financial problems, and unhappiness are not God's will. Christian Scientists, or students of Christian Science, will study the Scriptures and use Mary Baker Eddy's book as a guide and commentary. They hope to achieve a spiritual mind set that will allow them to discern and enjoy God's will for their lives and that will bring about mental, spiritual, and physical health. The Church of Christ, Scientist, discourages it members from seeking medical care from physicians. Instead Christian Scientists rely on Jesus' promises of healing.

The Church of Christ, Scientist, does not observe baptism or Communion; and it does not have an ordained ministry. Local congregations are branches of the Mother Church, the First Church of Christ, Scientist, in Boston, Massachusetts. Each congregation elects lay leaders to preside at worship services and to conduct the business of the church: First Reader, who reads from Mary Baker Eddy's works, and Second Reader, who reads from the Bible. The Mother church also trains and licenses Christian Science practitioners who help people in their studies and pray with them during times of illness or distress. All offices of the Church are open to both men and women.

Worship services are the same in all branches of the Churches of Christ, Scientist. Worship includes hymn singing, special music, prayers, and readings from *Science and Heath* and the Bible. Christian Scientists stress the quiet dignity of their services and their church buildings.

The Church of Christ, Scientist, does not publish membership statistics. However there are approximately 2,500 branch churches in 68 countries.

For Further Reflection

Use the following questions as discussion starters:

What is your understanding of God?

If God is mind, what is God like?

The Bible says that the disciples healed people. Can people be healed today? Can we heal other people? Why? Why not?

What is the relationship between prayer and healing?

Does your congregation read from sources other than the Bible? Does it consider other sources authoritative?

Can books other than the Bible be God's Word? Why? Why not?

The Church of Jesus Christ of Latter-Day Saints (The Mormons)

As a teenager and as an adult, Joseph Smith had visions. In 1820, angelic messengers convinced him that all contemporary churches and creeds were not only wrong, but an abomination to God. Later he received golden plates and instructions about how to interpret them; they became the *Book of Mormon*. (The name *Mormon* was given to Smith and his followers by outsiders. While they do not reject the name, Mormons prefer to be called Latter-Day Saints.) In 1829, three apostolic visitors conferred on Smith the authority to build the "true church." So the Church of Jesus Christ of Latter-Day Saints was born. From additional revelations, Smith wrote and published *The Doctrine and Covenants* and began to revise the Bible.

The Church of Jesus Christ of Latter-Day Saints grew quickly, but Smith and his followers encountered persecution wherever they went. In 1844, Joseph Smith and his brother were murdered. Because of further persecution and internal power struggles, most of the Latter Day Saints moved west under the leadership of Brigham Young and eventually settled in Utah near the Great Salt Lake. Smaller groups migrated to Wisconsin and Pennsylvania, and some stayed in Missouri. In 1896, Wilford Woodruff, Young's successor, gained statehood for the Latter Day Saints' territory of Utah. Today there are over 4.4 million Latter Day Saints in nearly 10,000 congregations. In Canada, there are 130,000 Latter Day Saints in about 400 congregations. About one-fifth of all Latter Day Saints live in the State of Utah.

Organization

In the Church of Jesus Christ of Latter Day Saints, local congregations are called wards. Congregations are organized into larger groups called stakes. The president of the church is considered a prophet and a seer, as well as a source of divine revelation. Latter Day Saints believe that God speaks directly to the president in order to guide the members of the church. The president and two counselors form the First Presidency, which is assisted by the Council of the Twelve Apostles. The Mormons have two orders of lay priesthood, into which almost all men are ordained; the priesthoods are closed to women.

Latter Day Saints' Beliefs

Latter Day Saints understand their goal to be restoring the true church of Jesus Christ. They are one of several groups that are part of the Restoration Movement.

All over the world, Latter Day Saints have temples that serve as the sacred centers of their communities; the temple in Salt Lake City is the most famous. Only Latter Day Saints in good standing may enter a temple where the rituals of celestial marriage and baptism of the dead are performed.

The church recognizes marriages for time on earth and also celestial marriages for all eternity. Not everyone is required to enter into a celestial marriage, but many do so. At death, men who have entered into celestial marriages, lived a righteous life on earth, and fulfilled all the ordinances (rules of conduct) of the church may become gods of their own worlds in the celestial kingdom, the highest level of heaven.

The church believes that baptism by immersion by a Latter Day Saint is necessary for exaltation, which is the highest state of being in the celestial heaven. Latter Day Saints have become excellent genealogists because they believe that through a proxy, who is a baptized Latter Day Saint of at least twelve years of age, they can baptize dead relatives who were not Latter Day Saints.

The church encourages everyone to tithe and asks young men and to a lesser degree, young women, to spend two years in volunteer missionary service. About half of the men and five percent of the women enter missionary service, which they must finance themselves.

Latter Day Saints have a firm belief in the family and in having children. Women are called to serve the church and their husbands and to share their husbands' priesthood. Mormons discourage the use of tobacco, alcohol, tea, and coffee.

Sacred Texts

The Book of Mormon is understood as another Testament of Jesus Christ. It recounts the belief that people came to prehistoric North America when the Tower of Babel was built and that others came shortly before the Babylonian captivity. According to the Latter Day Saints, Native Americans are the direct descendants of the ancient Hebrew people. *The Book of Mormon* also says that the resurrected Jesus came to America to preach the gospel to the descendants of the people of Judah and Israel. Most Latter Day Saints consider the *Book of Mormon* superior to the Bible.

Joseph Smith wrote *The Doctrine and Covenants,* which includes special revelations given to Smith by God, and *The Pearl of Great Price,* which contains the Articles of Faith and Smith's autobiography. The president of the Latter Day Saints can receive special revelation from God, so the interpretation of Smith's publications can and has been changed or altered by the president.

Are Latter Day Saints Christians?

Though they disagree with some important aspects of traditional Christianity, most Latter Day Saints consider themselves Christians, but not Protestants. They do not interpret the Bible in a way consistent with classical Christianity; and they reject key components of classical Christianity, such as the traditional natures of God and Jesus Christ, the concept of the Trinity, the doctrine of original sin, the traditional concept of the kingdom of God, and the doctrine of salvation by faith in Jesus Christ. They claim to be the only legitimate church of Jesus Christ. Therefore, they are not Christians in the same way as Roman Catholics, Eastern Orthodox, and Protestants are Christians. As a rule, the Church of Jesus Christ of Latter Day Saints does not cooperate with other churches.

The Reorganized Church of Jesus Christ of Latter Day Saints

After the death of Joseph Smith in 1844, a dispute occurred over leadership of the Church of Jesus Christ of Latter Day Saints. Some Latter Day Saints believed that Joseph Smith intended his descendants to lead the church. Most of the Latter Day Saints followed Brigham Young to Utah, but a small group remained in Missouri under the leadership of Smith's family and later became the Reorganized Church of Jesus Christ of Latter Day Saints.

Members of the Reorganized Church reject the name Mormon and do not adopt all the teachings of the Latter Day Saints in Utah. They do not believe in celestial marriage, baptism for the dead, or specific teachings about the Godhead. Although the church still uses the *Book of Mormon,* its theology more closely resembles traditional Protestant theology. The Reorganized Church permits the ordination of women into the priesthoods and cooperates with other churches. There are 150,000 members of the Reorganized Church of Christ of Latter Day Saints in 1000 congregations in the United States, and over 1,000 members in over 80 congregations in Canada.

Adapted from "Families of Faith: The People Called Mormon," *The Magazine for Christian Youth!,* February 1992, © Copyright 1992 by Cokesbury.

For Further Reflection

Use the following questions and activities to reflect on the key points in the article.

ORGANIZATION

➤ Tell the group to review the information about the structure and leadership of the church. Then ask these questions:

Who are the leaders of your church? Do women hold key positions in your local church? in the regional or national church?

In what way is the leadership of your church like that of the Church of Christ of Latter Day Saints? How is it different?

SACRED TEXTS

➤ Review the information about the writings of Joseph Smith. If possible, obtain a *Book of Mormon* from your local library and invite the group to compare it with the Bible. Then ask these questions:

What makes Scripture authoritative for you? Why do you accept one sacred writing rather than another?

Does God give faithful people new revelations that would be sufficient cause to change the Bible? Why? Why not?

Should other writings be considered sacred? Why? Why not?

LATTER DAY SAINTS' BELIEFS

➤ Tell the group to review "Latter Day Saints' Beliefs." The beliefs of the Latter Day Saints are complex; if possible, consult your local library for more information. Then discuss these questions:

What is celestial marriage? How does it compare to the concept and practice of marriage in your church?

Do you believe that people remain married or have a continuing relationship in heaven after death? Why? Why not? (See **Matthew 22:23-33**.)

What is the practice of baptism in your church? How does it compare with baptism in the Church of Jesus Christ of Latter Day Saints? What do you believe about baptism?

What does it mean to be a member in good standing in your church?

Are there buildings in your church in which some activities are permitted and others are not?

What are the circumstances in which you would not be able to enter a church of your denomination? to participate in the activities or worship at your church?

How do you feel about restrictions that would prevent you from participating in the life of the church?

Jehovah's Witnesses

Jehovah's Witnesses are a twentieth century religious group founded by Charles Taze Russell. He, along with Joseph Rutherford, Nathan Knorr, and Frederick Franz, formed the organizational and theological framework for what would become a worldwide religion.

Disenchantment and Prophecy

Russell came from a Presbyterian and Congregational background, but found himself increasingly disenchanted with the doctrine of his church. He was an avid student of the Bible, but came to reject traditional teachings on the Trinity, the second coming of Christ, and the existence of hell. What claimed his attention was biblical chronology and prophecy. Russell and the other three leaders regarded both Protestants and Catholics as apostate and declared that Jehovah's Witnesses were the only true Christians.

They created a religion fired by prophecies of the second coming of Christ, complete with specific dates and requirements for salvation. When the dates passed without incident, the prophecies were reinterpreted to show the errors in calculation and to project the next date.

The Work of the Few and of the Many

Witnesses believe in governance by a few. Their world headquarters in Brooklyn, New York is governed by fourteen to eighteen men who preside over decisions that affect all Jehovah's Witnesses worldwide. Since they speak for Jehovah and Jehovah cannot be questioned, their authority is not to be challenged in any way.

Not only is governance by the few, but so is salvation. Witnesses believe that only 144,000 people (including the Governing Board) will achieve heavenly salvation. (They base their projections on a literal reading of **Revelation 20**.) Other faithful Witnesses, the other sheep, will receive a restored and cleansed earth at the end of time, but will not reside or reign with King Jesus in heaven.

The way to achieve salvation is to be an active and effective missionary. All Witnesses have an obligation to evangelize door to door, to distribute the Witness writings, and to bring in new members. They are trained for this ministry.

Careful records are kept at the New York headquarters to keep track of every hour of each person's missionary activity. Ten hours a month is the required minimum. An auxiliary pioneer will work sixty hours a month and a regular pioneer about ninety. The time spent in proselytizing has a direct bearing on the quality of a Witness's afterlife.

Jehovah's Witnesses believe that Jehovah, the one and only person of God, created Jesus as the Archangel Michael, who created everything else. Jesus' life force was transferred from heaven to Mary, and he was born a perfect human being. Unlike traditional Christianity, Jehovah's Witnesses do not believe that Jesus was the incarnation of God or the messiah. Rather, he was anointed, at his baptism, as Jehovah's high priest.

Witnesses and the Bible

Jehovah's Witnesses are discouraged from reading the Bible by itself. Charles Taze Russell was a prolific writer; his works included *Studies in the Scriptures*. Russell concluded that if a person read the Bible alone, he or she would be destined to find only the darkness. By reading *Studies in the Scriptures*, with or without the Bible as a companion piece, a Christian could find the true light.

Witnesses believe that the Bible is the ultimate source of authority for life, and they accept their own translation, *The New World Translation of the Holy Scriptures*. They consider the Bible an organizational book that can be understood only in light of the organization of Jehovah's Witnesses. *Studies in the Scriptures; The New World*

Translation of the Holy Scriptures; and other publications of the Watchtower Bible and Tract Society, such as *The Watchtower* and *Awake!*, provide the basis for study.

Witnesses' Beliefs

Jehovah's Witnesses believe that Jehovah, the one and only person of God, created Jesus as the Archangel Michael, who created everything else. Jesus' life force was transferred from heaven to Mary, and he was born a perfect human being. Unlike traditional Christianity, Jehovah's Witnesses do not believe that Jesus was the incarnation of God or the messiah. Rather, he was anointed, at his baptism, as Jehovah's high priest. At the Resurrection, Jesus, who was now a spirit Son, was raised to heaven; his physical body was removed by Jehovah, and he returned to his identity as Michael.

The end times claim much of the Witnesses' attention. Through a complex series of biblical interpretations, they have predicted the dates of the beginning of the heavenly era and the chronology of the end times: the reign of Jesus Christ after the Resurrection, the victory of Jesus over Satan at the heavenly battle of Armageddon, the presence of the 144,000 elect who will exist forever with Jehovah and Christ in heaven, the existence of the faithful Witnesses in paradise on earth, and the total destruction of all other people.

Witnesses believe that Satan is to be feared, especially while he is in control of a sinful earth. Witnesses reject false religions (any religion other than their own), political involvement of any kind, honoring national symbols, military service, sexual temptation, and blood transfusions. Prohibitions against honoring national symbols and military service have led to persecution in many countries, including the United States during the early part of the twentieth century.

Witnesses tend to think of themselves over against other religious groups. They focus on being a close-knit group and on taking care of one another within the family and the Kingdom Hall. They operate no hospitals, nursing homes, or educational institutions. Although Witnesses will go to doctors and hospitals for care, they refuse blood donations and transfusions even if they would die without them.

Jehovah's Witnesses are interracial, interethnic, and deeply committed to ministry. Witnesses are strongly encouraged to maintain a healthy lifestyle and are discouraged from using alcohol, other drugs, and tobacco, or from yielding to any influence that might prompt immoral sexual behavior.

There are an estimated 914,000 Witnesses in just under 10,000 Kingdom Halls in the United States and 106,000 Witnesses in over 1,300 Kingdom Halls in Canada.

For Further Reflection

Use the following questions and activities to reflect on the key points in the article.

THE WORK OF THE FEW AND THE MANY

➤ Distribute paper and pencils. Ask the youth to draw an organizational chart of their denomination and local church.

➤ Invite the group to review "The Work of the Few and of the Many" and to compare their charts with the Witnesses' organization. Discuss these questions:

How is your church organized? Who is in charge? How is the structure of your church like that of the Jehovah's Witnesses? How is it different?

Who speaks with authority for your denomination? How do you feel about the way your church is organized?

What voice do you have in your church? What are the requirements for having a voice in the church? for membership in the church?

What effect does church membership have on your salvation?

JEHOVAH'S WITNESSES AND THE BIBLE

➤ Ask the youth to review "Witnesses and the Bible"; discuss these questions:

What version of the Bible does your church use?

In what ways is the Bible important in the life of your church? What materials are provided for Bible study?

WITNESSES' BELIEFS

➤ Divide the class into four small groups and ask each group to review one of the first four paragraphs in "Witnesses' Beliefs." Then each group should discuss the following questions:

What is the belief described in the paragraph you read?

How are the Jehovah's Witnesses' beliefs like your church's beliefs? How are they different?

How does your church deal with questions or concerns about doctrine or with challenges to authority?

➤ Bring the groups together to talk about what they learned. Ask:

Do you agree with what the Jehovah's Witnesses believe? Why? Why not?

Do you think the Jehovah's Witnesses are a Christian religion? Why? Why not?

Seventh-Day Adventist Church

Adventism is belief in the imminent return of Christ to earth. The Adventist Movement has appeared several times in the history of the Christian church. Most people who emphasize the imminent return of Christ belong to conventional Christian churches. However, in the first half of the nineteenth century, Adventism became a strong force in religious thinking.

William Miller, a lay Bible student, began the first Adventist movement. The movement began in existing congregations with people who took a renewed interest in the Advent of Christ. It was not Miller's intention to form a separate group.

Miller calculated from Scripture the precise time of Christ's return; he set the date between March 21, 1843 and March 21, 1844. When the year came and went with no Day of Atonement, a second date was calculated; and it too passed quietly. Many followers were disappointed and left the movement after March 21, 1884. More returned to their former churches when the second date passed. However, some of the Adventists continued to meet for further Bible study and ministry. The largest and most successful groups became the Seventh-Day Adventist Church.

The Seventh-Day Adventists are known for conducting their worship services on Saturday, but the Saturday observance is not unique to them. The Jewish Sabbath or day of rest is on Saturday (from sundown Friday to sundown Saturday). There is a Seventh-Day Baptist tradition as well, and many Roman Catholic and Protestant churches conduct services on Saturday evenings.

The Seventh-Day Adventist communities stress obedience to all of God's laws in both the Old and New Testaments. They adhere to many Old Testament regulations, such as some of the dietary regulations, in addition to the Ten Commandments. Seventh Day Adventists abstain from coffee, soft drinks, tobacco, and alcohol. Otherwise, the doctrines and practices of the Church are similar to conservative evangelical Protestantism.

Faithful Adventists believe in tithing, giving the church ten percent of their income. Tithes support both the day-to-day administration and the missions of the church.

Government of the denomination is connectional. Local congregations are organized into conferences that appoint local pastors. There are approximately 750,000 Seventh-Day Adventists in 4,300 congregations in the United States and 42,000 Seventh-Day Adventists in over 300 congregations in Canada.

For Further Reflection

Use the following questions and activities to reflect on the key points in the article.

➤ Invite the youth to look in a concordance for references to the Day of the Lord. Discuss:

Does your church look forward to a particular day or era when Christ will come again?

On what day or days does your church conduct worship?

When is your sabbath? Why is it on that day? Does it matter what day the church celebrates the sabbath? Why? Why not?

What are the Ten Commandments? How important are they in your church?

Does your church emphasize tithing?

What does your church say about giving? about money? about gifts and talents?

Easy Reference

Glossary

JUDAISM

GEMARA is one of the early (seventh century, C.E.) records of the oral tradition of the Torah. The Mishnah and the Gemara form the *Talmud* (Learning), which has been the basis for legal, philosophical, and ethical thinking in Judaism.

KETHUVIM is the Writings, thirteen books of various literary genre in the TANAKH.

MISHNAH, written around the third century C.E., is the first codified version of the oral tradition of the Torah. It contains ethical and ritual teachings.

MIDRASH is the interpretation of and commentary on the written scriptures.

NAVI'IM is the writings of the Prophets, twenty-one prophetic books in the TANAKH.

RABBI is a person who heads a synagogue or a temple and leads its worship and study. The Jewish faith has no priesthood.

SYNAGOGUE is the house of worship of Orthodox, Conservative, and Reformed Jews.

TALMUD is a sacred book of the Jewish faith. It contains the traditional interpretations of the Jewish laws, which are found in the Hebrew Bible.

TANAKH is the thirty nine books of the Hebrew Bible. The consonants in TANAKH stand for the names of the three parts of the scripture: Torah, Navi'im, and Kethuvim. TANAKH is also known as the Written Torah, and its Hebrew texts are treated with great respect.

TORAH is the first five books of the Hebrew Bible. The Torah teaches about the covenant and contains the fundamental principles of the faith: hope, justice, love, purity, thanksgiving, and virtue. It is believed to have been revealed to Moses at Mt. Sinai.

CHRISTIANITY

APOCRYPHA, which means hidden, or *Deuterocanon*, which means second law, is a collection of writings that date from about 300 B.C.E to about 200 C.E., the intertestamental period.

ASSUMPTION is a Roman Catholic and Orthodox belief. When Mary, the Mother of Jesus, died, she was not buried but was taken bodily to heaven.

BAPTISM is a sacrament, a sign of God's grace. The person baptized is recognized as a member of the church of Jesus Christ. Many Christians believe that the person baptized receives the gift of the Holy Spirit.

C.E. means Common Era, the period of time after the birth of Jesus. B.C.E., Before Common Era, refers to the time before the birth of Christ.

CHARISMATIC refers to a person who has had an experience of God's grace and has been given gifts of the Holy Spirit, such as speaking in tongues.

EPIPHANY means manifestation, especially the manifestation of God in Jesus Christ.

EPISCOPAL and EPISCOPACY refer to the leadership of bishops or a form of government in which bishops lead the church in particular geographic areas.

EUCHARIST means thanksgiving. It is one of the sacraments celebrated in Christian churches and uses bread and wine as symbols of the broken body and shed blood of Jesus Christ. The Eucharist is also called Holy Communion or the Lord's Supper.

GLOSSOLALIA means speaking in tongues, a spiritual gift given during prayer or a personal experience of God. Glossalalia is part of Pentecostal worship.

GRACE is the undeserved favor and blessing of God, freely given and received.

IMMACULATE CONCEPTION is a Roman Catholic belief that states that Mary, the mother of Jesus, was also conceived and born without bearing the original sin of human beings.

INSPIRATION and INERRANCY OF SCRIPTURE means that the writers of the Bible were guided by God and that therefore the text is the *inspired* word of God. Because it was inspired by God, it is also *inerrant*, without error, and is completely trustworthy and authoritative for the faith community.

MARY, MOTHER OF GOD, is the title Roman Catholics and Orthodox Christians use to refer to Mary, Jesus' mother. Since Jesus is the Son of God and equal to God, Mary is therefore the Mother of God and deserves special veneration.

ORDINANCES are a part of the ritual and worship of religious groups but are not considered sacraments. Ordinance means command.

PERPETUAL VIRGINITY is a Roman Catholic and Orthodox doctrine that states that Mary remained a virgin throughout her life.

SACRAMENTS are signs or means of grace that Jesus commanded his disciples to continue. Almost all Christians observe Holy Communion and Baptism. Roman Catholics and Eastern Orthodox include five other sacraments. Penance is an act of confession and pardon; Anointing the Sick, an act of confession, pardon, and blessing for the sick, was previously called Extreme Unction or last rites. In Confirmation, the individual publicly announces his or her faith and receives the gift of the Holy Spirit. Marriage is a covenant between a man and woman. Ordination sets apart the clergy and identifies them as representatives of Christ in ministry.

SAINTS, in the Roman Catholic and Orthodox Churches, are regarded as holy people who have the power to intercede with God on our behalf. Most other Christians think of the saints as the faithful members of the church.

SOLA SCRIPTURA is a Latin phrase that means Scripture alone. Martin Luther and the other reformers taught that Scripture, and only Scripture, was the final authority in matters of faith.

TRINITY refers to the idea that God is one in three persons: Father, Son, and Holy Spirit. Generally, the Father is identified as the Creator; the Son is God in the flesh, Jesus Christ; the Holy Spirit is the abiding presence of God in and for the Christian community. The Holy Spirit guides us and calls to our minds the teachings of Jesus.

ISLAM

IKHWAN means Brothers and refers to the Puritan movement in Islam.

JIHAD is Holy War. In the first few centuries of Islam's history, Jihad was understood as the war against heretics and infidels. Today, the word has a spiritual meaning: the war against sin and evil. Some regard Jihad as the sixth pillar of Islam.

MOSQUE means kneeling place and refers to the house of prayer for Muslims.

MUHAMMED was a human being chosen by God to be the last and greatest prophet or apostle.

MUSLIM means submitter, a person who submits to the will of Allah and an adherent of Islam.

PILLARS OF ISLAM are the five major practices of the faithful Muslim: Confession that Allah is the only God and that Mohammed is his messenger; prayer according to a particular ritual; fasting; giving, especially almsgiving; and the pilgrimage to Mecca if health and other circumstances permit.

QUR'AN, or Koran, means recitation. It is the holy book of Islam, which is true only if printed and read in Arabic. To translate the Qur'an into another language is an affront to Islam.

SHI'A, or Shi'ite, means partisans of Ali. It is the largest minority sect of Islam and the state religion of Iran. Shi'ites believe that all leaders of Islam should be descendants of Muhammad. Ismailis, who are members of a branch of Shi'a, are considered extremists. Baha'i, another offshoot of Shi'a, is now a religion in its own right. Baha'i teaches that all religions have the same source, that there is truth in all religions, and that religion must work with science to make a better world. Baha'i also emphasizes the importance of education and free thought.

SUFI is the mystical and devotional side of Islam that teaches the possibility of union with God.

SUNNI is the branch of Islam that accepts the Sunna, the tradition and the way of life that is normative for Muslims.

HINDUISM

BRAHMA is Brahman revealed as God the Creator.

BRAHMAN is the one, true, All Reality, the impersonal All Soul. Brahman is known to us in the form of gods and goddesses.

KARMA is both the evil and the good a person does. Karma determines destiny. If a person has done too much evil, he or she cannot escape the wheel of life or the transmigration of souls. If a person's karma is good, he or she will attain moksha or Nirvana. Both Hindus and Buddhists believe in karma.

SHIVA is the Destroyer, a god associated with both death and birth or rebirth. He is second only to Vishnu in popularity.

TRANSMIGRATION OF SOULS refers to the cycle of the soul through birth, suffering, death, and rebirth. It is caused by the inability of the soul to become one with Brahman. It is often incorrectly called reincarnation.

UPANISHADS are the Hindu writings in which the doctrines of maya and Brahman are explained.

VEDAS are the hymns and poems of the Hindu scriptures.

VISHNU is the savior god of the Hindu religion. Vishnu, the most popular of all the Hindu gods, often appears on earth as Krishna.

YOGA is the practice of a religious discipline for the purpose of achieving union with Brahman. The most popular is bhakti yoga. One who practices yoga is a yogi.

BUDDHIST

BODHISATTVA is a Mahayana saint who postponed entry into Nirvana in order to help mortals in their search for salvation.

BUDDHA is the title of Siddhartha Gautama in Theravada. In Mahayana, Buddha is the title of any enlightened deity.

EIGHTFOLD PATH is a way of believing, being, and behaving that provides the answer to alleviating the suffering of all humankind and leads to sainthood and Nirvana.

ENLIGHTENMENT is sudden insight into true understanding of the Four Noble Truths.

FOUR NOBLE TRUTHS were discovered by the Buddha through enlightenment. These truths form the basis for a Buddhist worldview: All people suffer from unfulfilled and inappropriate desires, but suffering can be overcome by following the Eightfold Path.

MAHAYANA means great vehicle and refers to the majority of people following Buddha. In Mahayana, the community includes not only monks but laity; and the laity can also achieve Nirvana.

NIRVANA is a state of peace and enlightenment that involves being unaware of one's self. It is freedom from desire and the sufferings desire causes. Nirvana can be attained by following the eightfold path.

THERAVADA refers to the minority of the followers of the Buddha, who are also the closest to his teachings.

TIPITAKA is the name given to the Theravadan scriptures, which, along with two others, are also accepted by Mahayana.

VAJRAYANA is a name for Buddhism in Tibet.

Stats-at-a-Glance

These figures represent the membership of religious groups in North America (the United States and Canada) or the World. Some churches keep careful records; others do not, so membership statistics may be approximate. The figures represent all the denominations in each religious tradition even if they are not all discussed in the text.

Total Population	North America 289,000,000	World 5, 642,000,000
Buddhist	565,000	334,002,000
Hindu	1,285,000	751,360,000
Jewish	6,850,000	18,153,000
Muslim	3,332,000	1,014,372,000
Christian	241,147,000	1,869,751,000
Roman Catholic	97,892,000	1,042,501,000
Orthodox	6,062,000	173,560,000
Anglican	7,404,000	75,847,000
Protestant	97,176,000	382,374,000
Protestant/Other	**United States**	**Canada**
Adventist	782,363	42,083
Baptist	36,417,404	359,698
Brethren	54,829	4,008
Christian Church (Disciples)	1,011,502	4,066
Christian Churches and Church of Christ	1,070,616	7,500
Churches of Christ	1,726,872	7,181
Episcopalian/Anglican	2,471,880	848,581
Friends (Quakers)	109,771	1,095
Jehovah's Witness	914,079	106,052
Latter-day Saints	4,582,850	141,111
Lutheran	8,382,667	292,945
Mennonite	258,856	94,172
Methodist	13,704,500	23,650
Pentecostals	9,572,274	261,517
Presbyterian	4,233,895	234,156
Reformed/United	2,072,414	2,095,072